Adam Bird is no-one really.

He's not famous. He hasn't achieved an

or ground-breaking. He doesn't teach

education institution. He's not smart in the use of social media and marketing.

Adam, with his wife, leads a small but growing congregation as part of a larger church in the South-West of the United Kingdom.

What he does have going for him is his deep love for God and his desire to see lives transformed by the freedom that comes from truly understanding the Gospel of Jesus Christ.

He is also passionate about effectively communicating Bible truths to a searching generation.

He is the author of more than zero books (this is his first!), and he lives with his family in beautiful Dorset, where they also serve their local community                as                Foster                carers.

# Resilience

Finding the Strength to Thrive when Life Sucks

Adam Bird

FAB LIFE

ISBN: 978-1-5272-7758-8

Cover photo by: Marian G Ruggiero (Courtesy of Unsplash.com)

This book is dedicated to my amazing family,
who continually inspire me to be a better man.

To Fru, my wife –
I definitely punched above my weight when I got you.

To Gideon, JJ, Charlotte, Grace and Eliza –
I am thankful every day for the amazing privilege of being your dad.

# Contents

# Introduction

This year has definitely been the strangest of my life.
By a long shot.

I am a Pastor and Minister to a growing church campus that is part of a larger church body in the South West of the United Kingdom.

As a leader in Sunnyhill Church, it regularly falls to me to deliver (hopefully) uplifting and thought-provoking, bible-based messages to my congregation on a Sunday.

At the start of this year (2020), my thoughts were turned to the subject of 'Resilience'. I wanted to equip our church to be stronger, more courageous, more confident, more equipped to deal with the various troubles that life inadvertently throws at us.

My approach to this series was fairly 'generic'. I talked about general financial troubles, generic health issues, undefined relational problems and provided universal biblical and faith-based answers to these wide-ranging troubles. Little did I know that the troubles were about to become extraordinarily specific.

As I'm sure most of you reading this will be aware, a few weeks into this year saw the rise of the global pandemic – Covid 19 – which led this country and most other countries around the globe into lockdown.

Fear soared.
Financial troubles exploded.
Health issues rocketed.
Relational troubles multiplied.

The need for resilience seemed and still seems more important than ever. However, because of lockdown, the church building closed its doors and my 'delivery mechanism' for the 'Resilience' series was lost.

Hence, this book.

I have never written a book before so here, at the outset, I ask for your mercy and forgiveness for my lack of a decent grasp of the English language.

My amazing wife, Fru (who has a much better grasp of our mother tongue) has helped me refine some of the language and many of the points. Any good stuff that you find in these pages is likely due to her input.

All the other stuff – that's on me.

I hope and pray, as you read on, that you find the tools to grow in resilience and faith, and that you learn to make delicious lemonade with the       lemons       that       life       drops       in       your       lap.

# Chapter 1
# See-Saw

*Be strong and courageous. Do not be afraid; do not be discouraged,*
*for the Lord your God will be with you wherever you go.*
*Joshua 1:9*

Everyone has a breaking point.

Or so conventional wisdom (and countless movies) would tell us.
We've all seen *that* scene where the 'goodie' has been captured by the
'baddie' but is refusing to divulge the secret information. The bad guy
leans in, close to our hero's face and with terrible breath seeping
through his crooked, yellow teeth announces:
"You will talk. Everyone has a breaking point!"
(In other words - I'm going to keep on monologuing until you get an
opportunity to get the upper hand or escape from my evil
clutches...cue maniacal laugh)

Despite this being a spy movie cliché, we all know there is an inherent
truth in this statement.
*Everyone has a breaking point.*
No one is immune to difficult circumstances. Everybody comes face to
face with suffering at some point in their life, whether it's self-inflicted
or simply the natural circumstances of life.

*****

An extremely wise person once said the following statement to his
closest friends just a few short hours before reaching his own 'breaking
point';

*"In this world you will have trouble."*[1]

That's a pretty helpful clue about what we should expect in this life.
Trouble.
And plenty of it.
An alternative translation of the same sentence reads like this;

*"In the world you have tribulation and trials and distress and frustration;"*[2]

Were you expecting something different?
Maybe you thought (like many people do) that becoming a Christ-follower and surrendering your life to him made you immune from the troubles, hassles and difficulties that life in this world brings. Perhaps you thought (or were possibly even told) that if you decided to accept Jesus into your life, as your saviour, then your life would be free from trouble and would only consist of perfect relationships, uplifting conversations, no health issues, no bills, no anger or sadness, no more jealousy, temptation or impure thoughts.
How's that working out for you?
Probably the same as it's working out for me.

However, don't give up now.
That same wise man had a few other things to say. In fact, hot on the heels of that sentence about 'trouble', he said the following:

*"In this world you will have trouble. But take heart! I have overcome the world."*[3]
*(emphasis mine)*

There's a 'but'. And it's a big, beautiful and important 'but' that changes everything…

*****

When I left University as a fresh-faced, young, and naïve 21-year-old, my very first job was for a bank in the centre of London's Financial District. It was at the point in time where 24-hour personal banking was just beginning as a concept, but the internet wasn't yet widely available. So, the general public were being encouraged to do their banking activities by telephone. My job was to answer the phone in a courteous manner and help the customers with whatever they needed doing. In fact, the very first day all the trainees were taught the following statement:

"Certainly I can help you with that!"

We were taught that this phrase should be employed at every conceivable opportunity within every telephone call. It was a statement designed to leave the customer feeling 'looked after' and 'in control'.

But what If the customer happened to ask us something that we *couldn't* actually do? That's a great question! I remember asking my supervisor that very same thing. "Well," we were told. "In that case, you should *still* say, 'Certainly I can help you with that.'"
We wouldn't want the customer to not feel looked after or in control!
The key was to follow this positive statement with the word 'however'. And then explain in no uncertain terms why you certainly *couldn't* help them with that!

A conversation would go something like this: A customer would ask me to do something for them. E.g. "I want you to refund the charge you have made on my account immediately!"
To which my response was, "Certainly I can help you with that..." (short pause to help them feel looked after and in control) "However..." and then explain in the most positive and courteous manner possible why there was no way on God's green earth that that was going to happen!

We were emphatically instructed *never* to use the word 'but'. 'But' is not a sexy word (we were told) and should be avoided at all costs. If we used the word 'but' then there was a danger that the customer would not feel 'looked after' or 'in control'. We must always use the much softer word, 'however'.

This was drilled into me during my 2 weeks training period and then over the next 3 years I followed this script on hundreds of telephone calls per week.

So, what's my point?

This is more than 25 years ago now, however, I still feel a jolt when I hear or see the word 'but' used in a sentence instead of the gentler word, 'however'.

The truth is, there are some amazing passages and scriptures in the bible that contain this connective; 'but', including the scripture mentioned previously about *trouble* and *peace.*

This word 'but' is such a loaded word – it's a concept that has such power. (I was going to call this section, 'Big 'Buts' of the bible' but it somehow didn't seem appropriate!)

However(!), I have learned to love these 'buts' – let me give you some life-changing examples:

*For I am the least of the apostles and do not even deserve to be called an apostle, because I persecuted the church of God.* **But** *by the grace of God I am what I am, and his grace to me was not without effect.*[4]

*My flesh and my heart fail;* **but** *God is the strength of my heart and my portion forever*[5]

*Like the rest, we were by nature deserving of wrath.* **But** *because of his great love for us, God, who is rich in mercy, made us alive with Christ[6]*

*For sin shall no longer be your master, because you are not under the law,* **but** *under grace.[7]*

In every case, it starts with a premise.
A truth.
A weighty and troubling concept.
This is how it is.
This is the hopeless mess we're in.
We are deserving of God's wrath.
We are messed up sinners.
But…

*****

Imagine a seesaw.
As a young child, we had a seesaw at our local park and my sister would invite me on one end and she would sit on the other end. She was older and heavier than me so I would go way up in the air, with my legs dangling.
Totally Stuck.
I can't get off because it's too high.
Stranded and out of control.
Upset because I can't get down.
She is sitting on the other end grinning up at me because she has all the power.
But…
then my dad notices what's going on and he calmly walks over.
He doesn't tell my sister off.
He doesn't punish her.
He simply sits on my end of the seesaw.
And now this game is fun!

9

That's what a big 'but' does. (sorry dad!).

It's like this…

You are at one end of the seesaw and the weight of all these negative and difficult truths are at the other end.

Trouble that is heavier than you can handle.

Leaving you helpless and dangling.

It's an impossible situation…

But…

Then your dad notices your trouble.

He sees the hopeless situation you are in.

He comes over to help.

He's on your side.

It's not even that He balances it out. Your Father comes and sits with you at your end of the seesaw, and all those weighty troubles no longer hold the same power over you.

In that scripture I mentioned at the start, Jesus is letting his followers know that they should *expect* trouble (tribulation, trials, stress, frustration). This is a theme that's repeated again and again throughout the whole of scripture. Every single one of the giants of faith mentioned in the bible – Abraham, Isaac, Jacob, Joseph, Moses, Joshua, Gideon, Ruth, David, Isaiah, Jonah, Peter, Paul, The Apostles, the list goes on and on, all experienced difficult circumstances.

These were not Muppets.

They didn't have weak or ineffective faith.

They accomplished amazing things and were close to God.

And yet, they all experienced hardship and trouble.

A lot of trouble.

Sometimes even trouble of their own making.

Sound like your life?

Yep. Mine too.

*****

I've written this book as an encouragement to all of us to not spend our lives trying to avoid the natural (and unnatural) troubles of life. Yes of course there are both wise and foolish choices available to us every moment of every day and I hope that all of us are able to make the kind of decisions that help move our life forward. However, the truth is, we can make *great* decisions and yet still find ourselves in difficult circumstances.

And that's okay.
I think we just need to be not so 'troubled' by that.

Maybe what we need is not less trouble.
But more peace.
Not fewer storms.
But a stronger foundation.
Not a difficulty free existence.
But greater **resilience**.

As you read through the following chapters, my prayer is that you will find helpful and practical strategies that create increased resilience to those storms of life.
That you will find strength to thrive when life sucks.
That you will be more prepared when the 'mess' hits the fan.
That Jesus' prayer will be answered in you:

*"I have told you these things, so that in me you may have peace. In this world you will have trouble. But take heart! I have overcome the world."*[8]

11

# Chapter 2
# Here Comes Trouble

*The righteous keep moving forward,*
*And those with clean hands become stronger and stronger.*
*Job 17:9*

At the time of writing, there's a new movie out called *A Beautiful Day in the Neighborhood* starring Tom Hanks as Mister Rogers. The movie focuses on the real-life person of Fred Rogers, an American TV personality who for three decades pioneered a TV show aimed at pre-schoolers called *Mister Roger's Neighborhood*.

In each thirty-minute show, Mister Rogers speaks candidly to his young audience (ages two through five) about the every-day aspects of life – including both good and positive stuff but also including more difficult topics such as sickness, difficult feelings and even death.

Fred Rogers dedicated his life to gaining an understanding of how children's minds work and worked hard to create a TV show that would instil a sense of emotional wellbeing into his audience.

There is a quote by Tom Hanks in the movie that is a direct quote from Fred Rogers himself:

*There is no normal life that is free of pain. It's the very wrestling with our problems that can be the impetus for our growth.[9]*

So often, the amount of resilience in our life is directly proportional to the amount of trouble that we have had to overcome.

Let me say that again (and make it bold!) because it may be the most important sentence in this book...

**The amount of resilience in our life is directly proportional to the amount of trouble that we have had to overcome.**

*****

Resilience.

It's such a great word.

So underused.

We often use words like courage, strength and faith and hope, which are all connected to resilience, but *resilience* as a concept, is found throughout the bible in numerous teachings and memorable bible characters.

The online Cambridge Dictionary defines the word *Resilience* as follows:

*the ability to be happy, successful, etc. again after something difficult or bad has happened.[10]*

One of Jesus' most famous and memorable stories comes right at the back end of The Sermon on the Mount[11]. Jesus has been teaching some amazing and challenging principles; new ideas that fly in the face of the conventional wisdom and teaching of the time. Using phrases like:

"You've heard it said *such and such*. But I tell you *such and such*"

He tackles subjects as diverse as blessings, persecutions, the law and righteousness, hatred and murder, adultery and divorce, praying, fasting, giving, anxiety, judging and hypocrisy.

The people listening to His teaching are both amazed and (I would imagine) overwhelmed by many of these concepts. Towards the end of the teaching, Jesus makes the following declaration:

*These words I speak to you are not incidental additions to your life, homeowner improvements to your standard of living. They are foundational words, words to build a life on.[12]*

Jesus is, in effect, saying, don't treat these words like just another teaching.

They are different.

They are important.

They are powerful

And they can truly change your life.

We need to know them and understand the power they contain.

We need to work them into the fabric of our lives.

These words will make a huge difference if we treat them correctly.

If we do something with them.

When Jesus teaches us to *forgive those who harm us*...

It's not just a nice sentiment.

It's a game changer.

It will make your life a whole lot better and a whole lot less bitter.

When he says *love your enemy*...(by the way, no one else on the planet was saying anything like this)

It will transform us as individuals.

And it will transform the world in which we live.

If we apply it.

When Jesus encourages us to *serve one another*

or *not to gossip*

or *be generous*

or *pray for those who persecute us*

These are not just snappy sayings to put on a fridge magnet (by all means get them printed on fridge magnets if you want). The truth is, obeying these instructions will make a massive difference to our daily lives. They are foundational principles to live by.

Jesus goes on...

*'If you work these words into your life, you are like a smart carpenter who built his house on solid rock. Rain poured down, the river flooded, a tornado hit—but nothing moved that house. It was fixed to the rock.'* [13]

That house sounds pretty resilient doesn't it?

*In this world you will have trouble.* [14]

The question isn't *whether* the storms of life will hit.
They *will* hit.
It's just a matter of 'when'.
It's a mathematical certainty. The storms are coming. Are you prepared? Are you resilient enough to stay standing?
Jesus' parable doesn't say that the wise builder built his house in a sheltered spot that would be free of storms. Tucked in behind a nice rock face where the wind and rains couldn't get to him. In fact, the wise builder *expected* storms. He didn't know when they were coming so he prepared for it. He thought to himself, 'In this world I will have trouble. I know the storms will hit me.
The rain will pour.
The river will flood.
The tornado will hit.
I don't know when or how.
Right now, my world is peaceful and my view is amazing – I can see for miles and it's hard to imagine any trouble at all.
My kids are all doing great at school.
My marriage is in a fantastic place.
I love my work.
My finances are in good shape and my bills are covered.
But I know it isn't always going to be like this.
I need to prepare for the storms by building my life on something substantial.
Something strong and unmoving.

I need solid foundations.

The second builder sees things a little differently. He sees the same view as the wise builder. He thinks to himself, 'My life/marriage/kids/finances are great. Nothing to worry about here. What could possibly go wrong? I can simply enjoy this moment without any regard for the future.'

*'But if you just use my words in Bible studies and don't work them into your life, you are like a stupid carpenter who built his house on the sandy beach. When a storm rolled in and the waves came up, it collapsed like a house of cards.'15*

Unfortunately, this is a stance that many of us take. We think that a trouble-free life is the norm. We decide (perhaps not consciously) that <u>no</u> trouble *is* life. When we do experience trouble of hardships or difficulties or something that doesn't go the way we expect, that this is a deviation from 'normal' life.

*****

Remember the Mister Rogers quote at the start of the chapter? About the fact that there is no normal life free of pain?

The atheist-turned-Jesus-follower, C.S. Lewis explained it like this:

*I have been in considerable trouble over the present danger of war. Twice in one life—and then to find how little I have grown in fortitude despite my conversion. It has done me a lot of good by making me realise how much of my happiness secretly depended on the tacit assumption of at least tolerable conditions for the body: and I see more clearly, I think, the necessity (if one may so put it) which God is under of allowing us to be afflicted—so few of us will really rest all on Him if He leaves us any other support.16*

The truth is that we don't need to be living a trouble-free life in order to be living the 'life in all it's fullness'[17] that Jesus promised.

Life is life.

Trouble and no trouble.

Storms and peace.

If we expect trouble, we can prepare for it. We build solid foundations into our life – like the wise builder – to make us resilient when trouble hits.

In this particular parable Jesus was saying the way to build a strong foundation, the way to prepare for the storms of life (which are definitely coming) is by reading the word of God (the Bible) and applying it to our lives. Allowing those words to build us and shape us and prepare us for what's ahead.

The 'Word of God', applied directly to our life and to our circumstances creates resilience – like a house built on a rock. We are able to live with *confidence* in our decisions because we know that they are based on eternal truths and universal principles. Reading the Bible and applying it to our lives doesn't mean an end to all our troubles, but it does mean we can face our troubles, confident that the trouble has not come about from poor choices. When we make good choices, whatever the consequence of those choices, we will live without any sense of regret, and we know that it is the *regret* from poor decisions far more than the natural difficulties of life that bring us down and prevent us functioning with resilience.

*****

The biblical character - Job, was a man who faced incredible difficulties despite living a 'good' life. Much of the writing in the book of 'Job', is Job himself defending his choices and his actions to his friends who are all convinced that the calamities that have fallen on him are a result of poor decision making and a lack of humility before God. Wow. With friends like these, right...?!

*'The righteous keep moving forward,*
*And those with clean hands become stronger and stronger.'*[18]

Job here is speaking of people who make 'right' decisions. People who have based their choices and actions on something solid and unchanging and therefore they have fewer regrets. This is really the essence of resilience. The ability to keep moving forward - whatever comes your way, and as far as Job was concerned, this ability comes from making right choices and not from a trouble-free or pain-free life.

I have discovered that we become 'stronger and stronger' as our lives are lived more in line with the Bible. When our decisions are rooted in the grace and truth found in scripture then our regrets will be fewer and our resilience increases. The troubles around us may not be diminished but they will feel smaller and they will certainly have the power to affect us less and less.

# Chapter 3
# I Can't Do It

*Many are the plans in a person's heart,*
*but it is the Lord's purpose that prevails.*
*Proverbs 19:21*

Over recent weeks I've been watching the 'Rocky' movies with 2 of my older kids; JJ and Charlotte.

Now I love the character of Rocky Balboa, played brilliantly by Sylvester Stallone.

He's not the brightest candle on the cake.

He's not the sharpest knife in the drawer.

He's often not as strong as his opponents.

By all accounts he's not even the best boxer compared to his adversaries.

But what does come across in all the fights, in all the movies, is Rocky's Resilience.

Yes he gets knocked down again and again.

His face is mashed up.

He can hardly see through his battered and swollen eyelids.

His body is bruised and he's hurting all over.

Mick, his trainer, is standing ringside wanting to throw in the towel.

But Rocky is resilient so he gets up - again and again and again. And in every film (spoiler alert) he eventually overcomes his opponents. (except in the first movie – when the judge's decision goes to his opponent, Apollo Creed – shame on them!)

It's the kind of film that really gets your blood pumping. When watching these movies, you get to see a different side of people. It's amazing having your sweet-natured, 16-year old innocent daughter sitting next to you on the couch screaming "Hit him Rocky!!"

One of my favourite films in the Rocky franchise is the fourth movie.

Cleverly called – Rocky 4.

In this movie you have the character of *Ivan Drago*, a Russian super athlete who is crafted and trained (and, it turns out - drugged) to be stronger, bigger, fitter and faster than everyone on the planet. In a friendly exhibition bout near the start of the movie, he actually defeats Rocky's best friend *Apollo Creed*, who, in possibly the saddest moment in cinema, dies from his injuries, thus setting up an East v West showdown right in the middle of the cold war.

Cue – The montage!

Cutaways of our hero, Rocky, training in a back-to-basics, snow-covered barn, lifting horse carts, chopping logs and running through waist deep snow. All the while watched over by KGB agents. These shots are intermingled with various scenes of Drago in his high-tech training facility, watched over by scientists and trainers with computers and lots of flashing lights, injecting various drugs and looking very serious. And all this is set to the familiar 'Getting Stronger', music score[19].

What more could a fan ask for?

And then, right before their final fight – Drago looks Rocky in the eye (kind of - he's about 3 feet taller so actually Rocky, our vertically challenged hero, is looking at his belly button) and declares in his thick Russian accent - "I must break you!"

It's a wonderful, mouth-watering baddie moment.

The fight progresses and for 14 rounds, as expected, – Rocky is getting pulverised as Drago does everything in his power to make good on his promise to 'break him'.

But Rocky doesn't break.

Every time he is knocked down, he gets back up again. And in the 15th round, (I don't want to spoil the ending but…) surprise surprise…Rocky wins!

Cue – Bruised and battered Rocky, grabbing the mic, looking into the TV camera and screaming for the whole world to hear, "I love you Adrian!"

Sometimes love wins! YIPPEE!!
Sometimes, life CAN feel great and peachy and everything is going our way. We feel like we have hardly a care in the world.

But the truth is, there are other times when it seems like life is towering in front of us, looking us squarely in the face and saying, "I must break you".
I have those times and I'm sure you do too.
So what do we do with that?
Jesus tells us that we're going to face trouble – so we know for certain we're not supposed to aim for a trouble-free life. So, what *do* we do?

We need to build resilience into our lives. We need to approach those difficult moments with a transformed mind. With renewed thinking. With a strategy that will help us not just overcome the troubles, but to thrive in them. After all, it wasn't Rocky's intellect or physical prowess that brought him victory, it was his determination and character.
His resilience.

*****

There is a great biblical character from whom we can learn much, and we discover him fairly near the beginning of our bibles, in the book of Genesis. Joseph's story is all about resilience. Here is a man who, despite good looks and a fairly privileged upbringing, faced serious trouble over a significant portion of his life. Some of it was trouble he brought onto himself (as a young man he had a habit of winding others up!), but a lot of it was trouble that the circumstances of life just dropped in his lap. But - and here's the real lesson in this - *all* of the trouble he faced transformed him, shaped him and prepared him to become the person he needed to become in order to fulfil God's purposes and plans for his life. Every hardship, every difficult moment, every injustice he faced – he remained steadfast and allowed it to mould him and shape his character.

Later in his life whilst talking to the very people who had been the source of most of his trouble, he made this statement:

*"Don't be afraid. Am I in the place of God? You intended to harm me, but God intended it for good to accomplish what is now being done, the saving of many lives."*[20]

Considering the scale of the trouble that Joseph had to face, that is a pretty huge statement. I wonder if we can look back at the difficulties and betrayal that we have had to deal with in our own lives and say something remotely similar. It takes a whole lot of pragmatism and, dare I say it, *forgiveness* to talk in those kinds of terms (more on this in a later chapter).

And yet, this is the very attitude that enabled Joseph not just to survive but *thrive* in his difficulties.

Joseph is essentially saying,

"The trouble that I've had to deal with,

the suffering you have caused me,

the circumstances that were telling me 'I must break you!'

24

God used those moments to shape me and re-create me and enable me not just to get through it, but to thrive in myself and to help others."

Numerous times in Joseph's story, we read the phrase; 'the Lord was with Joseph'. He is sold as a slave BUT the Lord was with him and even in all his troubles he begins to prosper. He gets wrongfully imprisoned BUT the Lord was with Joseph and so he experiences favour – even in his terrible circumstances.
Eventually, Pharaoh has a dream and discovers that this man Joseph has the prophetic ability to somehow interpret dreams, so sends for him from prison.

*"I've heard it said that you can interpret dreams."*

This is Joseph's chance – he's been in prison for 10 years now. This is his opportunity to put things right, to negotiate.
You scratch my back and I'll scratch yours.
I'll help you if you help me.
Yes of course I can interpret the dream - but first I'm going to need a TV in my cell, a reclining Lay-Z-Boy chair and maybe one of those nice Nespresso machines – chrome, with an added milk frother!

Of course, we all know that is not the line that Joseph takes. What does he say to the most powerful man in the world who is standing in front of him asking for his help? Four beautiful, amazing words that we all need to learn:

*"I can't do it!"*

This is a phrase we need to get comfortable using. If you are anything like me, then you can be a little bit self-sufficient. We love to try and dig our own way out of trouble. Trouble comes and we think, 'I can handle it. I can solve it. I can climb my own way out of this pit.' And there are definitely positive aspects to having this kind of attitude.

There is a measure of resilience when we face difficult situations in this way. However, this is the way of the world we live in:
God helps those who help themselves.
You can do it!
Find your inner hulk and smash your way out of disaster!

Particularly when it comes to people like me.
Can we be real here for a minute?
I know I can be exactly like this. Stubborn and self-sufficient. Things go wrong, trouble hits and I retreat into my 'cave' until I find the solution. Because saying "I can't handle this" is simply not manly enough!

I wonder if there's a better way.

A way that will help me become even more resilient. A way that will help us to not only get through the trouble, but to grow and thrive in the midst of the trouble. What should we do? We should learn to say those same four words that Joseph used.

*"I can't do it."*

I cannot fix this. I cannot see a way around this or through this. In other words,

I… need…help!

I'm not talking about having a pity party. I'm not saying we should just give up. I'm not suggesting that you abdicate all your responsibilities. When we say those four words, we are simply saying, 'God, I need you. Without you – there's no way, but I know that with you, there is a way…

And here comes another one of those huge and beautiful 'buts'…

*"I cannot do it," Joseph replied to Pharaoh, "<u>but</u> God will give Pharaoh the answer he desires."²¹*

This is such a brilliant way to build resilience.

I arrive at the end of what I can do and discover the start of what God can do through me. When I remove all of the pride in my own ability, it's at that point (and only when I've reached that point) that God can lift me up. We all know that:

*God opposes the proud*
*but shows favour to the humble²²*

And just in case we haven't yet understood this point:

*Let us then with confidence draw near to the throne of grace, that we may receive mercy and find grace to help in time of need.²³*

*So we can confidently say,*
*"The Lord is my helper; I will not fear; what can man do to me?"²⁴*

There is a confidence that we should carry when we approach God in our time of need. A certainty that is beyond our own abilities and placed firmly in the direction of a compassionate and gracious God.

I can't do it. But God…

*Humble yourselves, therefore, under the mighty hand of God so that at the proper time he may exalt you²⁵*

\*\*\*\*\*

27

All too often we think that we have to try and handle the trouble by ourselves. Why? Some misguided sense of pride perhaps? And the outcome of this is probably a certain amount of success. Maybe we do get through to the other side of trouble. But often, I think it leaves us as damaged goods. It leaves us like Rocky at the end of all his fights – just about standing up but all that remains is a physical and emotional wreck.

Having an - 'I'm going to fight it on my own' - mentality leaves us battered, bruised and too exhausted to keep going. The absolute best we can hope for is to get 'through the trouble' by the skin of our teeth. When actually, there is a better outcome available to us.
Just like Joseph – we can thrive!

*And we know that in all things God works for the good of those who love him, who have been called according to his purpose....*
*If God is for us, who can be against us?...*
*Who shall separate us from the love of Christ? Shall trouble or hardship or persecution or famine or nakedness or danger or sword?...*
*No, in all these things we are more than conquerors through him who loved us.*[26]

We don't just want to conquer our trouble – we can be *more* than conquerors. We don't want to scrape through those battles and those troubles, we want to grow.
We want to become stronger.
We want to be more resilient.

\*\*\*\*\*

Did you know that it's possible to be <u>fruitful</u> in your troubles? Not just to get through it, but to actually come out on top.
It's possible for the difficulties to make us more productive than we would have been without them. And I'm not just talking about 'character building'. (this is what my mum and dad would say to us

28

when we were growing up and going through a difficult season or facing something challenging –' it's character building!').

That is definitely part of the benefit...but I know that with God involved, there's more than that. We can actually thrive and be fruitful in our trouble.

So despite all his many troubles, that have been going on for decades, Joseph invites God into the situation and finds himself elevated to a position of power and influence within Egypt. He eventually gets married and has children.

In the bible - looking at the names that people gave their children tells us something about them. The name lets us know what they were feeling or going through in a given season. Our own children were given names that meant something to us.

We gave our firstborn the name 'Gideon' because the biblical account of Gideon in the book of Judges was instrumental in a significant turning point in our lives.

Our second born, 'JJ' (Josiah Jeffrey) means 'God Heals' and 'Peace from God' because he was born with a serious, congenital heart condition and we wanted to speak life every time we said his name.

Next we had Charlotte, whom, we believed would develop a Godly character; reflecting the best qualities of humankind (plus, I wouldn't let my wife call her Abishag!).

Our adopted daughter, 'Grace' – we didn't pick her name but she was definitely a gift from God.

And our final birth-child (please God!) 'Eliza', means 'promised' and 'my God is bountiful' – he gave us far more kids than we were ever expecting!

Anyway, back to Joseph. He calls his first boy 'Manasseh', which means 'to forget' because he says, 'God has made me forget all my troubles'.

And this is one approach to life... How many of us say just that – 'I just want to forget it all. I want to put it behind me and move on with my life.'

But then he calls his second son 'Ephraim', which means 'fruitful' because 'God has made me fruitful in the land of my suffering'.

There are some key words there. Did you spot them?

GOD HAS MADE ME...

We will only find the benefit (the fruit) in our troubles when we get God involved. When we say, "I can't do it" but with God, not only can I do it, not only can I get through it, I can actually thrive and be fruitful, not in spite of the difficulties, but because of the difficulties. I can't do it…but with God…

This is next level thinking. This is a resilient mindset.

Instead of looking for ways to forget or be freed from difficult circumstances. Look for ways that God can make us fruitful in our difficulties. Realising that we can be *more* than conquerors!

*****

As I previously mentioned, when I left University I worked for a bank for a few years. But I had trained as a musician - my degree was in Performing Arts. So whilst the job with the bank wasn't bad, I always felt an inner longing to be working in music. There came a point one day, when I felt that God was encouraging me to take a step of faith and become a composer – so, with my wife's blessing and much prayer, I took out a bank loan, bought a studio and became a musician/composer (more on this miraculous story later in the book).

I did this with reasonable success for a few years, released a couple of albums, but then felt it was the right time  to get more training, so I went back to University to complete a  Masters degree in Composing for Film and TV, fully expecting that this would open the door for me to be the next John Williams or Hans Zimmer!

For the next few years I worked as a composer and God supplied amazingly for me and my growing family. There were a number of times that I came close to 'The Big Break'. Various commissions came my way but never developed in the way I expected. To cut a long story short, the big break into film music that I was looking for never materialised.

To make matters worse, during the same period my hearing was deteriorating considerably (the result of a childhood illness), to the point when I could no longer hear well enough to record and mix my own compositions. I remember the difficult day when I spoke to Fru - my wife – about selling all my studio equipment on eBay.
It was hard moment.
Giving up on my dream.
Thinking I had failed.
Not knowing what the future would hold.

The amazing thing was that God had something even better for me than I could have imagined.  For the next 15 years I ended up lecturing in Composing for Film and TV at a London University and also being employed as a Worship Leader in my local church.

I know what you're thinking…

What kind of University employs a deaf Composition Lecturer?!
What kind of church employs a deaf Worship Pastor?!

Well done!
Those are the right questions!
These jobs eventually led on to my wife and I moving across the country to plant a new church Campus for Sunnyhill. Which is where we are now and which I wouldn't change for anything in the world – not even being the next Hans Zimmer! (just in case you are unaware – Hans Zimmer is one of the best film composers around today – Inception, The Dark Knight, Dunkirk, etc.)

Every time people have prayed for me - that my hearing would be healed (which is a lot of times) - and I haven't received healing, this verse always comes to my mind – Joseph naming his second son 'Ephraim' because 'the Lord has made me fruitful in my troubles'. Not in spite of my troubles or difficulties, but because of them! God is able to turn any seemingly disastrous circumstance into a victory – even when we cannot see how that is even possible.

As I become more resilient.
As I lean on Him all the more.
I become MORE THAN A CONQUEROR.

I love how the great British evangelist Smith Wigglesworth says it:
'Great faith is a product of great fights.
Great testimonies are the outcome of great tests.
Great triumphs can only come out of great trials,'

\*\*\*\*\*

Just to wrap up this chapter, we read at the very end of the book of Genesis that Joseph's father Jacob is on his deathbed and Joseph brings his two sons in for a blessing. It was standard practise at the time for the firstborn to receive a double blessing however, Jacob reverses his hands and places his right hand on Ephraim's head and his left hand on Manasseh's head. The bible tells us that, 'he put Ephraim ahead of Manasseh.' [27]

Maybe it's time for us to switch these two approaches around also. Perhaps we should stop trying to forget our troubles or waiting for the difficult circumstances to end. Maybe we need to realise that we can be fruitful in our troubles.

As we come to God, as we say that prayer - 'I can't do it – but God...', we will find ourselves more and more resilient to the troubles that hit us and be able to say, 'The rubbish and the troubles and the disasters that are intended to break me, God is going to use them for good. The Lord makes me fruitful in my afflictions and I am more than a conqueror.

# Chapter 4
# Finding Hope

*I pray that the eyes of your heart may be enlightened*
*in order that you may know the hope to which he has called you.*
*Ephesians 1:18a*

We began this book by looking at Jesus' words to his disciples, spoken the night before he was crucified.

*"In this world you will have trouble – but <u>take heart</u> I have overcome the world."*[28]

I love those two simple words – Take heart. They are words that transform the picture entirely.
Trouble? Yes. Difficult circumstances and seasons? Yes!
But…
Take heart.
Have courage.
Don't let the trouble you face get you down or trip you up.
Persevere.
Be confident.

At its core, this a scripture about confidence. It's not a confidence that stems from everything going your way. It's a confidence rooted in the fact that Jesus has overcome the world. It's not a confidence in my abilities, but in His. It's not a confidence in my ideas or solutions, but in His presence.

So, we can confidently say,

*"The Lord is my helper; I will not fear; what can man do to me?"*[29]

There are many scriptures and promises throughout the bible that inform and remind us to *have confidence, to be strong and courageous[30]*,
*to stand[31]*,
*to fear not[32]*,
*to have faith[33]*,
*to be assured of the hope we have[34]*.

These are instructions from God to His people and this idea should be a great source of resilience in our lives.

When we find hope, we find resilience.

No one would dispute that hope is an enormously powerful emotion. It is a strong force for creating resilience within us. There are many books, blogs and articles written by Doctors and Psychologists that explain how a small amount of hope can have a huge impact on the outcome of a situation. Hope imparts a sheer belief that you have the capacity to overcome the crisis that you are facing.

Hope is not simply a wish for things to get better, it is an inner certainty that what awaits just around the corner is better than what you are facing right now.

Hope is the conviction that, though your child is lying in a bed in the Intensive Care Unit, they will pull through. It's the belief that despite your dreams not having materialised in the way you expected, there is something even better awaiting you.

Hope is the ability to start over when your business has gone belly up. It's the unfaltering tenacity of the cancer patient who battles on, believing that they will be back on their feet soon. It's the single parent who has lost their job but knows that new (and potentially better) employment is just the other side of the job application in front of them.

Hope is the difference between life and death when circumstances look bleak. Hope is vital for survival and pretty much everyone who survives a life-threatening ordeal that appears (at least on the surface) impossible to overcome, will point to hope as the element that got them through.

*"…a little tomorrow can make up for a whole lot of yesterday"*[35]

We - you and I - can put up with a whole lot of trouble, when we have hope. Possibly right now, in this season you are going through, you are feeling the trouble, but are devoid of hope. If that's the case, then my hope, *and God's hope* is that you will find hope for yourself. I would love it if the words written in this book would help to build more hope in your life. However, in order for hope to be effective as an instrument that builds resilience, it's vital that it is placed correctly. We need to be certain that the person/outcome we place our hope in, is good for it. We need to know that it won't let us down.

In the book of Proverbs we read,

*'Hopes placed in mortals die with them;*
*all the promise of their power comes to nothing.*[36]

Interestingly, the word *mortals* used in this proverb is a translation from the Hebrew word 'adam'. So hey, don't put your hope in me!

Actually, this word can be translated 'man' or even 'humankind' (it's where the original name for Adam came from in the book of Genesis). What the writer is trying to say is, people will, generally speaking, let you down. However, the immortal, omnipotent, omnipresent, omniscient Father God is faithful and trustworthy and will not let you down.

A correctly placed hope (in our creator God) can forge a resilience in you that nothing this world throws at you can possibly make a dent in.

*****

Let's explore this idea a little further.

I want you to imagine what your life would look like if you had absolute perfect, one hundred percent confidence of the following three facts.

1. There really is a God.
2. He's the God who made heaven, earth and everything in all creation plus He also knows you personally and has numbered the very hairs on your head[37].
3. He has promised to be with you, to walk beside you every day, to never leave you or forsake you, through all your troubles.

Imagine what your life could be like if you had that kind of confidence. That kind of faith. That kind of *Hope*. A hope and a confidence based on an assurance that there is nothing you have to face without that God.

A hope that says when trouble hits you – I know this is bad right now, but I am believing that God will be with me whatever I am going through.

A hope that says when you face temptation – 'Wow I'm really struggling with this area. I don't know how I'm going to get through this. I don't even know how I'm going to avoid it...but I know God is going to be with me through it.'

Even when great things happen; you come into a windfall of money, you get that dream job, you land that boyfriend or girlfriend that you know is way out of your league (if you've met my wife, you'll know exactly what I'm talking about!*) We know that it's not just the troubles and the bad stuff that can trip us up in life. We need the kind of confidence and hope that says, God, I don't know why this amazing thing is happening to me but I'm going to trust you for the wisdom to deal with it. To keep making the right choices. To not lose sight of reality.

(*BTW – My wife is way, way, way out of my league!)


Imagine what your life would be like if that were the case. You just trusted God.


Fully - one hundred percent.
Absolute.
Perfect.
Confidence.


The confidence that helps you to say, 'God's got a perfect will for my life and I am wholly at peace with whatever happens.'
No anxiety, no fear about your kids, your marriage, your finances, your elderly parents, your jobs, your friendships, no stress about the floods creeping towards your home (at the time of writing this, the river that is about eighty yards from our house burst it's banks!).
It's not that everything is going your way – it's just you have confidence in your ability and in God's presence to see you through the difficult times, the great times, the normal times, every situation. Your peace is unshakable because of the confidence and the hope you have.


Okay so maybe that's not you. Yet. But maybe you know someone like that. Your parent or Your grandmother. I have a clear memory of my Nana (my dad's mother). She seemed to be like this. I don't remember ever seeing her angry or stressed. I never saw her lose her temper or rattled in any way. She was great to be around because she lived her life simply confident in God's goodness. (I possibly might be remembering her with rose-tinted glasses – that's okay – she's my grandmother and she was prone to wearing pale pink cardigans!)

Maybe you've seen terrible stuff happen to other people and it has shaken your faith. Perhaps you have been struggling on their behalf. And at the same time, they appear to be doing okay. And you're like, 'are you seeing what's happening right now?' And they're like 'yes, I'm seeing it, but God's got this. And I just have peace right now.'

How do they do that?!

So imagine that this could be your experience too. What if you really could, like King David say,

*The Lord is MY shepherd. I lack nothing….Even though I walk through the valley of the shadow of death I will fear no evil…'[38]*

I love the imagery in the second half of this Psalm.

*'You prepare a table for me in the presence of my enemies.'[39]*

This is the kind of experience we were talking about in the previous chapter.
Even though I'm surrounded by my enemies. Despite being encircled by troubles. Regardless of the fact that disaster has hit.
God has prepared a table for me.

Imagine a table filled to bursting with all your favourite goodies! A trifle. A banoffee pie. Chicken Biryani with Peshwari Naan bread. Ben & Jerry's Phish Food ice-cream. A big, juicy fillet steak.
Is your mouth watering yet? Can you picture the table?

From the outside looking in, all anyone can see is the trouble. All that's visible is the circle of enemies surrounding me. They can't see this amazing banquet that God has put out for me in front of my awful circumstances. God is helping us to thrive in our trouble. To be fruitful in our difficulties.

I think that this is where God wants to take us. He wants us to have that kind of resilience, that kind of hope, that kind of confidence, that level of *trust*.

Because trust is everything.

*****

Right at the beginning – this is the very thing that broke the relationship between God and man. God didn't say, 'here's a list of things to do. Good luck!' It wasn't that Adam and Eve managed most of it but tripped up on one or two and God said, 'sorry guys – you didn't quite cut the mustard.'
No – the whole thing broke down because Adam and Eve ultimately didn't trust God. They didn't trust that his will for them was for their best. The relationship break happened because they had a trust issue.

God has been working ever since to restore trust. To restore perfect confidence. Everything that God has done. Every story that we read about, the events that took place throughout the bible are all God demonstrating his faithfulness towards mankind. God is giving us something solid in which we can hope and trust. He is giving us a reason to be confident. He provides the means by which we can 'take heart'.

*****

I've realised that the more trust I have in a relationship, the better the relationship is. In my marriage, my friendships and my family, being able to say - 'I trust you completely. I trust that you will do what you say you're going to do. I trust you that you're not going to harm me. I trust that you've got my best intentions at heart in the decisions you make.' – this elevates my relationships to a whole new level.

At its core, the whole bible is essentially God calling humankind back into a trust (faith)-based relationship with him.

You could be someone who hasn't yet made a commitment to follow Jesus. You're seeking but you're not quite there yet. What's stopping you? Dare I say it's probably a trust issue? You haven't yet come to the place where you fully trust that God is who he says he is. Or that you are who He says you are. It's a trust thing.

You could be someone who has decided to follow Jesus but maybe there are some areas of your life that you are still holding back from trusting Him with. You've compartmentalised your life and you're not quite ready to fully jump into that deep end just yet.
I think that is true for many of us. Few (if any) of us have reached that place where we are fully trusting and hopeful and confident in every single area of our life. How do I know this? Because our lives would look so different to how they look right now.

*****

There is an incident we read about in the Gospel of Matthew about a man who surprises Jesus by his trust. It's the account of the Roman Centurion who approaches Jesus and asks for healing for a servant. We read about it in Matthew chapter 8.
Jesus is walking through the town of Capernaum, doing the usual stuff; healing people, feeding people, just hanging out with his posse, casting out evil spirits and stuff. His day is interrupted by a man – probably dressed in his full uniform, with his helmet (complete with brush top – I never understood why their helmets had that bushy thing going on) – He's probably flanked by a number of soldiers and looking quite

intimidating. I expect everyone is a bit nervous as the soldiers approach. I can imagine Matthew leaning over to Peter and whispering, 'what have you done now? Have you forgotten to pay your taxes again?'

But the centurion, as bold as you like, walks right up to Jesus and asks for help. There are two things here that Jesus was fully aware of and that we need to bear in mind too…

1. The Romans are the bad guys in first century Judea. The invaders. You don't want anything to do with these guys. They have the power to drag you away and you're never heard from again (e.g. Jesus' cousin John).

2. The Romans are pagan, law breaking and don't generally have any connection with the God of the Jews

*"Lord," he said, "my servant lies at home paralyzed, suffering terribly."*[40]

Let's take a step back here and try to imagine this scene. Your worst enemy. Not just your enemy, but as far as you're concerned, the enemy of God has just walked up in the middle of the street, in full view of everyone, asking for help.

I can imagine the disciples turning away and doing an imaginary high five with each other. 'The servant of the Roman soldier is suffering? Good!'
They're not going to say it out loud but in their heads they are probably thinking, 'Great! – I hope your servant dies a horrible death and I hope you catch whatever he has, and you and all your men die a slow, painful death too! Come on Jesus – let's go and heal some Jewish people.'

But Jesus has something else in mind.

*"Shall I come and heal him?"*[41]

WHAT?!

Time out Jesus.

Do you know what you're saying?

Have you lost your mind?

But Jesus is totally serious. 'Shall I come to your home to heal your servant?'

Because we all know that's how healing is done. Jesus comes and lays hands on the one who is sick and then they get better.

*The centurion replied, "Lord, I do not deserve to have you come under my roof."*[42]

The disciples whisper to each other, 'Ain't that the truth!'

*"But just say the word, and my servant will be healed."*[43]

Well this is new.

The Centurion says, in effect, Jesus, you don't need to come to my home. I've seen what you've been doing. I've heard how you've done these amazing miracles. I think you don't even need to touch my servant. I think that you don't even need to come to my house to do it. I think you can send this miracle wirelessly across town.

This is a whole new level of trust. And then he explains why he thinks this...

*For I myself am a man under authority with soldiers under me. I tell this one, 'Go,' and he goes; and that one, 'Come,' and he comes. I say to my servant, 'Do this,' and he does it."*[44]

The Centurion, in effect is saying, 'Jesus – you and I are the same. We have this in common. I have these men under me – my one hundred soldiers, and if I order them to do something, they do it without questioning. If I tell them to jump, they say 'How high?' If I tell them to guard a prisoner throughout a freezing cold night – they obey without a second thought.

I have authority over these men, not because they respect me. Not because I'm special. Not because I pay them. I have authority over them because of the position given to me by Rome. I represent Rome – and that gives me authority.

Now I have seen that sickness and death and demons do what you say – so you obviously represent something higher too. I don't know whose authority you are under – you don't look that special – you're just a guy like me – but these things do what you say just like my men do what I say. And I'm confident that the authority you represent is big enough and strong enough to heal my servant all the way across town at my home. From right here.'

*When Jesus heard this, he was amazed and said to those following him, "Truly I tell you, I have not found anyone in Israel with such great faith*[45]

Jesus is amazed at the Centurion's understanding. The word 'amazed' is a translation from the Greek word 'Thaumazo'. This is a word found throughout the New Testament and is applied to many different people – the crowds, the religious leaders, the disciples. – This is the only time that it is applied to Jesus. You might almost say that this is a new emotion for Jesus – He is astonished, surprised and astounded at what this Roman Centurion has just confessed to him.

This is also a huge 'diss' to all the Jews there – the religious leaders, the disciples, everyone. I can imagine that they are all standing there thinking, 'by all means tell us we need to have more faith – but please don't compare us unfavourably with this pagan Roman!'

Jesus is like, 'You guys need to pay attention to this heathen soldier –
he gets it! He gets it in a way that I haven't ever seen before anywhere
in God's chosen people.

Why does he get it? He trusts me. He has confidence in me. Because of
who I represent. He understands that I am the representation of God
the Father, the creator of all things. The one who has power of
sickness and disease. The one who has overcome the world.

In this world, you will face trouble.
You will face sickness and hardships and difficulties.
But take heart, have trust, be confident, FIND HOPE, I have
overcome the world.
I have ultimate authority over everything you are likely to face.'

The Roman Centurion found hope in a God like that.

Imagine if we truly believed and found hope in a God like that too.

*****

Without God our hope is insecure.
With God our hope is based on something solid. Our resilience is
greater. Our confidence is strong because it is on something
immovable and unshakeable…

*When God made his promise to Abraham, he backed it to the hilt, putting his own
reputation on the line. He said, "I promise that I'll bless you with everything I
have—bless and bless and bless!"*
*Abraham stuck it out and got everything that had been promised to him. When
people make promises, they guarantee them by appeal to some authority above them
so that if there is any question that they'll make good on the promise, the authority
will back them up.*

*When God wanted to guarantee his promises, he gave his word, a rock-solid guarantee— God can't break his word. And because his word cannot change, the promise is likewise unchangeable.*
*We who have run for our very lives to God have every reason to grab the promised hope with both hands and never let go.*[46]

*We have this hope as an anchor for the soul, firm and secure.*[47]
(this confidence, this trust)

Trust in Jesus IS our anchor.
It is our confidence.
It is our hope.

It's easy to drift.
From God,
From your God-given purposes.
From your dreams.

The anchor is there to keep us from drifting. To keep us tethered to hope. To make us more and more resilient.

*****

The following hymn was written by Priscilla Jane Owens more than a hundred years ago and I thought the rhetorical questions that it asks would be an appropriate end to this chapter and of course the answer to these questions (when your hope is in Jesus) is a resounding 'YES'!

*Will your anchor hold in the storms of life,*
*When the clouds unfold their wings of strife?*
*When the strong tides lift, and the cables strain,*
*Will your anchor drift or firm remain?*

*Will your anchor hold in the straights of fear*
*When the breakers roar and the reef is near?*
*While the surges rage, and the wild winds blow,*

*Shall the angry waves then your back o'erflow?*

*Will your anchor hold in the floods of death,*
*When the waters cold chill your latest breath?*
*On the rising tide you can never fail,*
*While your anchor holds within the veil.*

*Will your eyes behold through the morning light,*
*The city of gold and the harbour bright?*
*Will your anchor safe by the heavenly shore,*
*When my storms are passed for evermore?*

*Chorus*
*We have an anchor that keeps the soul*
*Steadfast and sure while the billows roll;*
*Fastened to the rock which cannot move,*
*Grounded firm and deep in the Saviour's love!*

Live your life as if God's promises to be with you always are true.
Find your anchor.
Find confidence.
Find hope.
Be resilient.

# Chapter 5
# It's Just Not Fair.

*Do not take revenge, my dear friends, but leave room for God's wrath, for it is written: "It is mine to avenge; I will repay," says the Lord.*
*Romans 12:19*

Where does your greatest trouble comes from?

Consider all the difficulties you face. The things you worry about most of all. The stuff that challenges your resilience above everything else. If you're anything like me, and I expect you are, the source of most of your trouble is other people. Right?

Let me allow you to enter into my world for a moment...
I don't like being late.
I really, *really* don't like to be late.
For anything.
In fact, you might say I'm a bit (a tiny bit!) OTT when it comes to arriving on time. And I get frustrated at people (i.e. my family) who make me late. It sometimes feels like they do it on purpose. Like I'm some weird, social experiment – 'let's see what happens if we make dad a few minutes late today!'

Sunday morning comes around. We have to set up church in the hall where we meet, and I need to arrive first with all the equipment. So, I tell my kids, "we're leaving at *this* time!" (which by the way, is the exact same time as we left last Sunday, and the Sunday before that, and the previous fifty Sundays!). *That* time comes around and some of them are still making breakfast, some of them are walking around half dressed, one of them is looking for his toothbrush (don't ask...). I'm standing by the front door huffing and puffing like a demented lunatic, pushing

49

everybody out to the car, counting them as they go to make sure I haven't missed anyone (I've literally done that before!), refusing to let them back in the house (even if they have forgotten their bible).

Okay, maybe I'm not as bad as all that but hopefully you can begin to understand my pain.

The truth is, I don't always respond as well as I might. Which isn't a great start for the Pastor on a Sunday morning. (Don't worry - God is still doing a work in me!)

I wonder what or who brings you the most trouble?

Parents – it may well be your kids.

Kids – it may be your parents. Or one of your teachers. Or a bully at school.

Perhaps you have a difficult neighbour or a boss who's an unreasonable, tyrannical megalomaniac with serious control issues (okay, maybe they aren't as bad as all that either).

Maybe the source of your greatest trouble is in the room you are in right now. Why don't you look up from this book and give them the dead eye? (Not really – don't do that, it won't help.)

The simple truth is, the moment that you are in relationship with another human, you're going to have challenges, difficulties and trouble. The deeper in relationship you are with them, the greater the potential for hurt and trouble.

My wife will tell you this is true!

People say and do things that hurt us and offend us and it's like each thing is another weight on us and these things can just build up and grow over time, getting heavier and heavier until we can't take another step and we crumble.

Or - we can be like a can of fizzy pop that has been shaken and shaken. Eventually the pressure is too much and we explode.

We need to learn what to do with all these hurts and offences so that they don't build up.

The one thing we can't do is ignore them and hope that they somehow just melt away.

*My people are broken – shattered! – and they put on band-aids, Saying, "It's not so bad. You'll be just fine." But things are not 'just fine'.*[48]

*"Mum's the word," I said, and kept quiet.*
*But the longer I kept silence*
*The worse it got— my insides got hotter and hotter.*
*My thoughts boiled over; I spilled my guts.*[49]

We can't just ignore these difficult feelings. We can't just park them at the back of our mind and think they will dissolve, like sugar in water, all by themselves. We can tell ourselves that everything looks okay on the outside and no one will know. But we know what's really going on the inside. Our resilience is, little by little, getting eroded away.

*****

Another glimpse into my world…

Most of the time, I'm a reasonable and calm guy. People who know me say I am pretty chilled.

Patient even.

If someone has upset me, you probably won't know it by looking at me.

But if I don't deal with it, inside it can be dark.

Really dark.

There's all this pressure building up.

I become more and more withdrawn as it plays over and over in my head.

It begins to affect my closest relationships.

51

I have conversations with myself about the person who has upset me, and if I don't deal with it, eventually it will just explode everywhere over some poor unsuspecting person who has just been a hair-trigger for all the inner turmoil.

Maybe you have been in a conversation with someone when they suddenly exploded over a really small thing. It's usually because there's internal pain and trouble that has built up over a period of time, that they haven't dealt with.

*****

So, what's the answer?
How can we increase our resilience against the trouble caused by people hurting us?
Does the bible have anything to say about this? – About the fact that people are our greatest source of trouble?

Perhaps the bible can tell us how to change everyone in the whole world so that they don't hurt us anymore?
Or maybe it can tell us how we can avoid those specific people that cause trouble in our lives?

Not so much.

Scripture's answer to trouble caused by other people is *not* to change others – but to shift the focus onto me.

To change me.

I know what's going on in your head right now.
You are thinking, 'that doesn't really seem all that fair. People are causing *me* grief and hurting *me* and giving *me* pain – and the bible's

answer is to deal with *me*? To shift the focus onto my reaction towards the people who hurt me?

Surely that isn't fair. Right?!

Here's a little secret for you that could change your life…

Fairness is overrated.

Let me say it again.
God knows, and what we all need to know is: fairness is overrated. It's not an essential aspect of life – despite modern opinion to the contrary.

Sometimes, when I ask my kids to help out with something, they will use this phrase; "it's just not fair! Why aren't you asking someone else?"
Maybe you have heard that same phrase in your home.

It's just not fair.

We can be so caught up in making sure that something is 'fair', that we completely miss the point of fairness. When we think a particular outcome is not fair, usually we are comparing ourselves to somebody who we think is better off than ourselves. When my children are complaining that I've asked them to help out, you can be sure they will compare themselves with the child who is not helping out, rather than the child who *is* helping out. And this is true for all of us, we like to compare ourselves to people who we think are better off than us rather than those who are not. When we are complaining that we don't have the latest smart phone, gaming console or gadget, we are more likely to compare ourselves to the people who do have those things rather than the people who cannot afford to even put food on their table.

We have a 'warped' and selfish definition of fairness.

*****

So how should I respond when I've been hurt? How I should act when somebody has shovelled a pile of trouble in my lap? How can I make sure that the trouble doesn't create bitterness or anger or resentment inside me? How can I deal with it in a way that makes me more resilient?

The first and most important step towards dealing with hurt and trouble caused by other people...is forgiveness. (Right now you might be tempted to flick straight to the next chapter because you've heard people talk about forgiveness in the past. I would encourage you to read on, even if you think you know all there is to know about it. It's amazing how easily that old rogue 'unforgiveness' can creep back into your life

Forgiveness – on the surface it's not very fair. But it is the *best* response to any hurt that someone has caused you.

*Get rid of all bitterness, rage and anger, brawling and slander, along with every form of malice. Be kind and compassionate to one another, forgiving each other, just as in Christ God forgave you.*[50]

Notice it doesn't say – remove all bitterness, rage and anger by avoiding people who give you those feelings....it says the answer is...to forgive them.

In this world you *will* have trouble. The potential for bitterness and rage, anger and malice is always going to be there, as part of the fallen world we live in and it's not going away anytime soon.

However, you can do something about it.

*****

This is amazing. We can actually do something about it.

One thing that resilient people have learned throughout the course of their life, is that it's almost *impossible* to control other people's behaviour. I wish people would act differently. I wish they wouldn't cause me the trouble that they do. But I can't control that.

What I *can* control is my response. I have complete control over how I react when someone hurts me. I can hold on to the hurt. I can let it fester. I can be like a can of coke, shaken up, ready to explode....

Or I can forgive. Let it go, so it let goes of me.

I like how theologian and author, Lewis B Smedes puts it:

*To forgive is to set a prisoner free; and discover that the prisoner was you.*

I can't emphasise enough the importance of forgiveness to enable us to live a free, resilient and God-centred life. It may not be fair but it's like a superpower when it comes to living the best life possible.

Peter was keen to get the whole forgiveness thing absolutely right, so he asks Jesus, "Lord, how many times shall I forgive my brother or sister who sins against me? Up to seven times?"[51]

Now it was rabbinic teaching of that day that a man should forgive up to three times. So Peter's feeling pious about doubling that and adding one for good measure. Seven times!

I'm sure that most of us know Jesus' answer, "I tell you, not seven times, but seventy-seven times."[52]
Essentially, Jesus was saying that forgiveness is unlimited.

Don't ever stop forgiving.
Don't put a limit on it.
It's a reply not based on fairness or the Jewish law but on God's grace.
We need to forgive *everything* that needs forgiving.

And Jesus doesn't leave it there. He explains this idea further by telling a parable about someone who doesn't forgive.

*****

There's a man who owes the king a ridiculous amount - Ten thousand talents. Bearing in mind that one talent is approximately twenty years wages, so ten thousand talents is equivalent to the wage of about four thousand lifetimes.
It's an impossible sum.
However, the servant begs the king for mercy and the benevolent king cancels the debt and lets him go.

So far, so good.

In this parable, the man who owes the king this outrageous amount, is me!
And you!

You see, one of the first principles of forgiveness is to understand the scale of the debt we have been forgiven. We need to have a true and proper perspective of the debt of sin that we each owed and that has been wiped clean.
It's beyond imagining.

This is actually the *good news* - the *gospel* - of Christianity. It's the Grace of God that meets us exactly where we are – warts and all – and says to us, "I want a relationship with you. But because I am a Holy God in whom there is no sin, and because you are an unholy people, full of sin, that relationship is impossible. It's totally impossible! Your debt is so huge, there is no way you can ever make yourself right with me.

There is no way you can pay that debt.

So, what I'm going to do is send my son, my perfect, sinless son. Who will willingly take on all your sin – and die in your place.

Now your sin is no longer be a weight around you. Your debt is cancelled – completely."

If we haven't fully understood and accepted the reality that, once we come to Jesus, we are totally and completely made free of the debt of sin, then we have not really understood and accepted what it means to be a Christian.

This is the ball game.

*****

As we read the bible. As we grow in the faith and in our discipleship. As our relationship with God deepens. As we relinquish control of our lives and learn to trust Him more and more, we begin to see ourselves as we truly are: Messed up - but forgiven and made free. It's interesting to see how Paul's perspective of himself changed over the course of time.

- In 48AD, he refers to himself as 'a servant of Christ'[53]
- In 55AD, he writes, "For I am the least of the apostles"[54]
- In 60AD, "I am less than the least of all the Lord's people"[55]
- In 64AD, "Christ Jesus came into the world to save sinners – of whom I am the worst"[56]

Taken at face value it appears that the apostle Paul was becoming a worse person over the years! It seems like he is on a downward trajectory! But the truth is, he is moving in the right direction. He was getting a Godly understanding of himself. His identity, more and more, became in line not with how people saw him, but how he saw himself in the light of God's grace and forgiveness. He is gradually understanding the amount that he had been forgiven, and the size of the freedom that had been paid for him by Jesus.

The same should be true of us. We have to understand the depth of God's forgiveness and mercy for us. Why? Because this will, in turn, underpin our forgiveness of others.

We forgive, because we've been forgiven.
Forgiving someone isn't *fair*. But it is *just* because we have experienced God's forgiveness for everything wrong that we have done.

**Forgiveness:**
**It's Just. Not fair.**

So, what happens next in Jesus' parable?

The servant – who has had this crushing debt forgiven, then remembers another guy who owes him a hundred denarii (one denari is about a day's wage. So one hundred denarii is about three months wages). He demands payment and then has the man thrown into prison until he could pay.

So, the servant, who had been forgiven four thousand lifetimes wages, refuses to forgive the man who owes him three months wages.

*Then the master called the servant in. "You wicked servant," he said, "I cancelled all that debt of yours because you begged me to. Shouldn't you have had mercy on your fellow servant just as I had on you?" In anger his master handed him over to the jailers to be tortured, until he should pay back all he owed.*
*This is how my heavenly Father will treat each of you unless you forgive your brother or sister from your heart.*[57]

It's essential that we bring whatever shadowy offences we are carrying, the trouble that people have caused us, into the light of the forgiveness that we have received.

And even more than that, Jesus says a number of times that his forgiveness of us is actually dependant on our forgiveness of others.

The simple truth is, if you are not able to forgive those who have caused offence to you, you can't possibly understand and receive God's forgiveness for you. It simply won't compute with you. How you treat others will directly affect how you yourself expect to be treated.

*****

One of my children, when they were younger, went through a season of walking around with their two favourite stuffed toys. A lamb (called 'lamby') and a flamingo (called 'Bermango'). She would hold on to these two toys as if her life depended on it and you if you tried to give her a different toy or anything else to hold, she couldn't do it because her little, chubby arms were already full.

And this is the reality we face. We won't be able to receive forgiveness if we are holding on to *unforgiveness* and *resentment*.

Unless you can forgive those who have hurt you, however badly, you will never understand and accept God's forgiveness for you.

Your life won't be free.

You will not walk in the grace of God.

Let me add a side note in here...

Forgiveness is not necessarily a lack of consequences. And it's also not about remaining in an abusive relationship. Sometimes, you need to forgive *and* walk away. And sometimes also, restitution needs to be made for an offence. However, if you're using unforgiveness as a punishment, that's just not going to work because it hurts you far more than it hurts them! Unforgiveness makes a lousy punishment. We need to let go and give it to God.

Do not take revenge, my dear friends, but leave room for God's wrath,…
for it is written: 'It is mine to avenge; I will repay,' says the Lord. [58]

This scripture is not about enjoying the fact that God is going to avenge, to punish the offender. It's not about praying, 'God, I forgive them but pour out your wrath. Smite them O mighty smiter!'[59]

The same passage goes on:

*On the contrary:*
*If your enemy (the one who has hurt you) is hungry, feed him;*
*if he is thirsty, give him something to drink.*
*In doing this, you will heap burning coals on his head.* [60]

I know that some of you are thinking, 'That's awesome - If I'm nice to them then God's going to set their hair on fire!'
Does that sound like the God of grace? No! To heap burning coals simply means to bring about repentance. Doing good will actually bring about a better result – a change of heart and attitude. That's what this is about.

People are going to do things that upset you or make you angry. We don't simply lose all our emotions when we give our life to Jesus. One of the best ways to overcome disappointment or anger is to forgive.

Maybe in your head you are thinking:
"That's all well and good Adam, but you don't know what they've done to me"
"That's fine but you don't realise what they have said about me"
"You don't realise the pain and anxiety this has caused me"

"They don't even seem sorry for what they did!"

You are right on all counts. I don't know what you have been through. But Jesus knew all about this. Remember what he had to suffer at the hands of people and his prayer on the cross; "Father forgive them, for they do not know what they are doing."

Every single story of true forgiveness has a pile of pain and hurt behind it.

Perhaps you are thinking to yourself, "As soon as he is remorseful..." or "As soon as I don't feel angry any more..." or "When she says sorry, then I'll forgive"

This may seem fair, but it is backwards.
**When we make forgiveness conditional, we are essentially handing control of our mental wellbeing to someone else.** The best way is to forgive first and let God heal us and do whatever changing work he needs to do in them.

Or maybe you are thinking, "I will forgive, but I won't forget!" I'm not sure that's the attitude that Jesus wants either. I would even question whether that is true forgiveness.

I heard a story of a couple where the man had messed up, but he apologised and they made up. However, every so often his wife would bring it up again and again. Eventually the man said to his wife, "Why do you keep bringing it up? I thought your policy was to forgive and forget"
"It is." She replied, "but I don't want you to forget that I've forgiven and forgotten!"

God talking through the prophet Jeremiah says: 'Their sins I will remember no more.'[61]

God has chosen not only to forgive our sins, but also to remember them no more.

*****

In my experience, when we truly choose to forgive offences against us, the Holy Spirit will also help us to let go of them. By God's grace a Christian can so forgive that every memory brings not bitterness but peace.

To finish this chapter let me tell you about a time when this made a real difference to me.

I have led a pretty blessed life. Really, I haven't had to endure much pain or hurt. However, about 20 years ago, somebody did something against me that was horrendous, the most painful thing that anyone had ever done. Not a physical pain, but I was hurt and devastated and pretty much crippled by it.

After a sleep-deprived night of worrying and plotting revenge, the next morning I decided on a different approach. So, I called the person and told them that I forgave them.

Now I'm not telling you this to make you think how Holy I am. There have been plenty of times when I haven't got this right and I've held on to unforgiveness and suffered for it. But this was just one time when I feel like I got it right.

Did it mean I was best buddies again with the guy? No of course not.
Did I feel better straight away? No. the healing took some time, but you will never convince me that the phone call I made that morning didn't get the ball rolling. I was able to begin letting go of the pain and hurt.

My resilience went up a notch that day.

Remember, often the healing starts with the words and the intentions. The feelings will follow after.

Forgiveness *is* hard. But it's a *superpower* when it comes to bringing us into freedom. We forgive much because we have been forgiven much more.

Forgiveness may not be fair, but it is the path to making us more resilient. Unforgiveness may *feel* fair – but it's the path to bitterness and resentment.

Forgiveness.
It's Just. Not Fair.

# Chapter 6
# The Trainers of Praise

*He has sent me... to bestow on them a crown of beauty instead of ashes,*
*the oil of joy instead of mourning,*
*and a garment of praise instead of a spirit of despair.*
*Isaiah 60:1,3*

Have you ever worn something that makes you feel special?

I remember getting my first pair of branded trainers.
It was my twelfth birthday and the whole family took me into Wolverhampton town centre to buy new clothes. My dad had a credit account with Burtons (a menswear chain) and he gave me a budget and let me loose in the store, but I knew exactly what I wanted. A pair of grey, Adidas trainers (I can't remember if they had a name or not – I was just dazzled by the fact that they were Adidas!).

You need to understand, we were not a particularly wealthy family, and there were a lot of us to feed and provide for. At the time my dad was working for a Christian Charity which meant not much money and rarely new clothes. Mostly I wore hand-me-downs from my older brother.
I spent the first eighteen months of secondary school wearing 'pumps' for school sports. Remember pumps? – The black, unbranded canvas ones with the elastic across the top and the orange soles (or if you were a little better off – Dunlop white lace ups!)

I can't begin to describe the ridicule I suffered.
The lack of self-worth I experienced.
How completely 'un-resilient' those black pumps made me.
Now, no more!

My school locker room 'trainer shame' days were finally over.

I was twelve years old and I now had a pair of real, honest-to-God Adidas. It was going to be my turn to laugh at the sad geeks wearing unbranded pumps.

I marched down the High Street that day a changed person. I'm pretty sure I wore those trainers out of the shop, all the way home and didn't take them off until bedtime. I felt like a king. I knew my 'pump' days were over and I couldn't wait for the next school sports lesson.

Now we all know that kids can be quite mean sometimes and if my memory serves me correctly, I'm pretty sure I got teased about the fact that my new trainers were not Adidas 'Kick' or 'Samba' (which were the height of trainer fashion in my school at that time). However, for a few halcyon days, I was on top of the world. My street-cred (in my own mind at least) had rocketed and I wanted the world to notice me, to accept me and even *like* me on the basis of my new, improved footwear.

*****

I'm pretty sure everyone at some stage has known that feeling. Strutting down the street like John Travolta (Saturday Night Fever reference - if anyone is interested) as if the world is your oyster. Whether it's because you are wearing a particularly nice item of clothing, jewellery or make up.

Or you're having a *great* hair day.

Or you have a new pair of Adidas trainers.

Something about the way you look, or what you're wearing makes you feel just great.

It makes you feel like you can handle anything that comes your way.

It makes you feel untouchable, resilient even!

Interestingly, I recently discovered a new word, 'Estrenar', that means exactly this. It's a Spanish word with no direct English equivalent and it roughly translates as the happy feeling you get from wearing a new item of clothing. That bliss and euphoria that causes people to max out their credit cards getting their next 'retail therapy' fix. At its root is a deep, human longing for acceptance and significance, and we all know that the feeling it produces is only temporary at best. You can probably guess how long my new-found 'estrenar' lasted. Just as long as it took for someone to stamp their muddy size nines all over them, or until my mate bought the next, latest, cool footwear.

*****

The bible actually points us to a way of experiencing that feeling more permanently. The 'trainers of praise' that never get dirty or out of fashion.

I love the prophecy in Isaiah chapter sixty-one that speaks of a reversal of Israel's circumstances. It is a prophecy of hope in a future day when the world will be put to right. It speaks of the coming of a Messiah who will turn things around, and in fact, hundreds of years later, Jesus stands in the Synagogue in his hometown, Nazareth, and uses this prophetic picture to describe himself, ushering in the start of his world-changing ministry.

The prophecy speaks about the poor, the broken-hearted, the captives, prisoners, mourners, grievers, wearing ashes and despairing spirits.[62]
It describes all kinds of trouble that people in this world face.
And it speaks about a future hope from the coming Messiah (Jesus):

*Good news for the poor,*
*binding up the broken hearted,*
*freedom for captives,*
*release for prisoners,*
*comfort for those who mourn,*
*provision for those who grieve,*

*a crown of beauty instead of ashes,*
*the oil of joy to replace mourning*
*and a garment of praise instead of a spirit of despair.*[63]

I love the whole imagery of transformation. Yes, there are things in this world that can bring you to despair. There is the shame and ridicule of not fitting in.
Of wearing the wrong footwear.
There is a long list of personal shortcomings we each have to live with. But that is not the whole picture. Remember the verse we began this book with?

*'In this world you will have trouble...* [64]

But that is not the whole picture either;

*'but take heart, I have overcome the world.* [65]

In our troubles, we can choose a different 'outfit'. We have been provided with a crown of beauty and a garment of praise to wear. We can strut in the midst of trouble (like John Travolta!). When circumstances or spiritual forces are pulling us down, making us captive, breaking our hearts, we can choose a different path. We can decide to change our thinking about ourselves. We can ignore own voice and the voices around us that would try to convince us we are less, and we can choose to listen to whom God says we are instead.
We can wear better clothes.
We can choose to praise.

To praise God in the midst of trouble is a choice and it's also often a sacrifice. We don't always feel like doing it

*Through Jesus, therefore, let us continually offer to God a sacrifice of praise—the fruit of lips that openly profess his name.*[66]

There are some key words in this verse that are going to help us build resilience through praise.

First, our praise should be to God and through Jesus. Jesus is our gateway to God's presence. He was the fulfilment of Isaiah's prophecy. He is the way, the truth and the life. No one comes to the Father except through Jesus.[67]

Second, our praise should be 'continual'. We don't praise simply when we feel like it. We praise in the good times, the sad times, the bad times, the battles and the troubles. That's why it's a sacrifice.

Thirdly, our praise is done 'openly'. We declare it and others hear it, or they see it in us. Praise is not just a private thing; "Oh it's just between me and God – I only do it on my own in the shower." There is a place for private worship of course but it should also be given publicly.

*I will praise you, Lord, among the nations;*
*I will sing of you among the peoples.*[68]

If we feel like we are lacking God's presence in our lives, then singing songs of praise and worship is a great tool for moving our hearts towards Him. All too often when trouble hits, we decide to wallow in our despair and let self-pity overwhelm us instead of choosing to put on the garment of praise. When we continually sing songs of praise to God, openly, through Jesus, not allowing our circumstances to define our experience of His presence, we are engaging in spiritual warfare. We do battle in the heavenlies and this results in a transformation here on earth.

We don't let the cloak of despair overwhelm us, instead we choose to put on a new garment that brings us back into His presence – the adidas trainers of praise!

*****

There's a great example of this in the book of Acts. Paul and his crew are ministering in the city of Philippi, when, over the course of a few days, a female servant who is evidently possessed by an evil spirit begins to follow them and shout at them. She keeps badgering them until Paul has had enough. He rebukes the spirit in the name of Jesus and it leaves her.

This lands Paul and Silas in a whole heap of trouble.[69] (By the way, trouble is not the exclusive domain of people who make poor choices. You can make great (even Godly) choices and still find yourself facing trouble and difficulties.)

Paul and Silas are sent before a magistrate who orders them stripped, flogged and thrown into prison. They are placed in the innermost dungeon and their feet are fastened in stocks.[70]

At this point, what would your response be? I'm pretty certain mine would be self-pity and despair. 'All I did was help a girl get free from an evil spirit!'. I think I might even have some 'choice' words directed at God about my predicament.

What do Paul and Silas do, bearing in mind they are probably naked, they've been severely flogged and they are chained up in cold, dark dungeon?

They choose a garment of praise.

The bible tell us:

*About midnight Paul and Silas were praying and singing hymns to God, and the other prisoners were listening to them.*[71]

70

In the most horrible of circumstances – bruised, broken, cold and uncomfortable – Paul and Silas are praising – openly. You might even say they are 'strutting' in their garment! They are not being coy about their faith. They are not being quiet and personal, whispering silent prayers in the darkness. They are declaring their love for God, loudly, so the other prisoners can hear them. It doesn't tell us exactly what they were singing, but I imagine it to be one of David's Psalms, crying out to God for deliverance, acknowledging Him as the source of their help and choosing to praise whatever the circumstances. For example:

*Save me, O God, by your name;*
*vindicate me by your might.*
*Hear my prayer, O God;*
*listen to the words of my mouth.*
*Arrogant foes are attacking me;*
*ruthless people are trying to kill me—*
*people without regard for God.*
*Surely God is my help;*
*the Lord is the one who sustains me.*
*Let evil recoil on those who slander me;*
*in your faithfulness destroy them.*
*I will sacrifice a freewill offering to you;*
*I will praise your name, Lord, for it is good.*
*You have delivered me from all my troubles,*
*and my eyes have looked in triumph on my foes.*[72]

David was a total ninja when it came to praise and worship. He understood the benefits of developing this habit of praising in all circumstances. There are real, tangible benefits for us when we learn to put on a garment of praise whatever we are going through.

*****

**In the Good times**

Of course, we can praise in good times - In the book of Exodus we read about The Israelite nation escaping from Egypt; crossing the red sea and then seeing their enemies swallowed up behind them. What do they do when they see what God has done? They sing a huge song of praise. They have a praise party;

Then Miriam the prophet, Aaron's sister, took a timbral in her hand, and all the women followed her, with timbrals and dancing. Miriam sang to them:

*"Sing to the Lord,*
*for he is highly exalted.*
*Both horse and driver he has hurled into the sea."*[73]

When good things happen we should praise. We should demonstrate our gratitude to God. This reminds us that He is the source of all the good things we experience in life, and He is the one to thank when we avoid the bad stuff that might have happened -after all, those horses and drivers weren't entertaining God's people with a diverting display of dressage!

There's a great Country & Western song by Tim McGraw. It's a song about God getting invited into ordinary life circumstances and turning things around. As each of the stories are told, the end refrain echoes out: 'Touchdown Jesus'.

*There was a little girl just down the street*
*They were prayin' for a miracle but runnin' outta hope*
*Some stranger was an angel and he gave her what she needed*
*You oughta see her today, that was ten years ago*
*Touchdown Jesus*[74]

When we praise God in the good times – we are, in effect, saying 'Touchdown Jesus'. We are acknowledging the source of all goodness and this prevents us from getting prideful.

It's great to praise God when everything's going well and when suffering is avoided or averted, however, true resilience is forged when we put on that garment when things are not going so well and life sucks.

*****

## In the battles

In the Old Testament book of Chronicles, we read about the nations of Moab and Ammon coming up to fight against the nation of Judah. This is a vast army for Judah to face and Jehoshaphat is 'alarmed'. He calls the nation to pray and fast, and God answers through a prophet;

*"Do not be afraid or discouraged because of this vast army. For the battle is not yours, but God's...Take up your positions; stand firm and see the deliverance the Lord will give you"*[75]

*Jehoshaphat bowed down with his face to the ground, and all the people of Judah and Jerusalem fell down in worship before the Lord. Then some Levites from the Kohathites and Korahites stood up and praised the Lord, the God of Israel, with a very loud voice.*[76]

*...Jehoshaphat appointed men to sing to the Lord and to praise him for the splendour of his holiness as they went out at the head of the army, saying:*
*"Give thanks to the Lord,*
*for his love endures forever."*
*As they began to sing and praise, the Lord set ambushes against the men of Ammon and Moab and Mount Seir who were invading Judah, and they were defeated.*[77]

This is a great example for us. When we are facing a potentially overwhelming battle – we should praise. Notice that they weren't singing, "Give thanks to the Lord, for He is about to annihilate our enemies! He will tear off their arms and legs and give us a great victory and we will scoff at their uncool trainers!"

They were praising God for his enduring love!

The idea wasn't to sing fighting words that geed themselves up and made them feel invincible as they went into battle. It is enough to choose to put on that garment of praise and sing about who God is. Finding the right combination of words and phrases is simply not as important as having the right heart.

When we are willing to praise God in the troubles that we face, we essentially offer Him a bigger portion of our conscious thoughts (the bible calls this 'magnifying'). And when we magnify Him, this gives us a better perspective on our situation.

*****

**In the apparent defeats.**

Perhaps you're thinking, 'That's all well and good Adam, but what about when it seems as if God hasn't defeated the enemy for us? What about when we are facing trouble day after day after day?'

I get it.

Sometimes God uses trouble and battles to grow our character. Do you remember the account of Joseph in chapter 3, who faced two decades of difficulties? He was misunderstood, hated, sold into slavery, wrongfully accused and forgotten, all of which made him into the person he needed to become in order to save a whole nation.

Similarly, in the Old Testament book of Daniel we read about Shadrach, Meshach and Abednego. Three bright young men who are torn from their home in Jerusalem by the Babylonian army. Now I imagine these three Godly men in their homes in Jerusalem watching the approaching Babylonian army and praying earnestly to God for deliverance from the invading army.

The invaders overrun Jerusalem, so I imagine them praying that they won't be the ones exiled to Babylon.

They are exiled to Babylon, so I imagine them praying that King Nebuchadnezzar won't make them worship the image he has created.

The King insists that everyone worships the image, so I imagine them on their knees praying that they won't get caught only worshipping Yahweh.

They do get caught and now I imagine they are praying that the King will relent and won't throw them into the furnace.

And now they are standing before the King and about to be thrown into the fire. What do they do? Surely, it's time to give up on the God to whom they have been praying so fruitlessly?

Not even close. Here's what they say:

*King Nebuchadnezzar, we do not need to defend ourselves before you in this matter. If we are thrown into the blazing furnace, the God we serve is able to deliver us from it, and he will deliver us from Your Majesty's hand. But even if he does not, we want you to know, Your Majesty, that we will not serve your gods or worship the image of gold you have set up.*[78]

Whatever happens to us now, despite all the difficulties that have gone before, we will *never* stop praising and worshipping the Most High God!

Not because we expect him to save us, but simply because He is the only one worthy of all our praise.

*I'm gonna sing in the middle of the storm*
*Louder and louder, you're gonna hear my praises roar.*
*Up from the ashes hope will arise*
*Death is defeated, the King is alive.*[79]

Even when we are in the thick of trouble and it seems like God is not answering our prayers the way we would want or expect, we can still choose to put on that garment (trainers!) of praise and let it take the place of the spirit of despair.

There are no circumstances in which praising God will not help us. At the very least, praising in the midst of trouble promotes resilience in us.

Even more than wearing new Adidas trainers!

I pray that we can all, like David, get to a place where we can say,

*I will praise the Lord at all times.*
*I will constantly speak his praises.*
*I will boast only in the Lord;*
*let all who are helpless take heart.*
*Come, let us tell of the Lord's greatness;*
*let us exalt his name together.*[80]

# Chapter 7
# The Blessed Life

*But blessed is the one who trusts in the Lord,*
*whose confidence is in him.*
*They will be like a tree planted by the water*
*that sends out its roots by the stream.*
*It does not fear when heat comes;*
*its leaves are always green.*
*It has no worries in a year of drought*
*and never fails to bear fruit.*
*Jeremiah 17:7-8*

The word 'blessed' is not used much in our society although it is used a great deal in churches. It can be perceived as quite a religious word and it can mean different things to different people. You've probably got your own idea about what it means to be 'blessed'.

I heard a story about a man who had been really good for years and an angel shows up and says, "Because you've been so good, God wants to bless you! You can choose either the blessing of wisdom, the blessing of good looks or the blessing of ten million pounds."

The man thinks for a moment, looks around at all his friends watching and replies with great gravitas, "I choose the blessing of wisdom".

There is a flash of lightning, a peal of thunder and immediately the man is transformed. Everyone is watching as he just sits there staring down at the table.

Eventually, one of his friends leans over and whispers through his teeth, "Come on. You've just been granted amazing wisdom. Share with us from your divine insight."

The man slowly lifts his head, looks around at his friends and announces, "I should have taken the money!"

Whether you think that's funny (Dad joke alert!) or perhaps a little cynical, for many people, having a 'blessed' life equates to possessing money and wealth or at the very least, having just a bit more financial security. We often compare our own life with other people's lives (or more accurately, our perception of their lives), and we conclude that our life is less blessed than theirs.

This is especially true when we compare our *real* life to everybody else's *fake* life; the life that is posted on Facebook or Instagram. It's important to remember that what we see on social media is only a snapshot of a shareable moment.

It used to be we would only get this snapshot once a year in the Christmas newsletter. Maybe you aren't old enough to remember the dreaded Christmas Newsletter. It would arrive on your doorstep at the beginning of December (just to demonstrate how fantastically organised they are) and would be one or two sides of bragging, interspersed with studio quality photos showing the family in a picture-perfect Christmassy pose:

*Your nephew Johnny has just passed his grade 8 clarinet and has been voted 'most likely to succeed by everyone in his school. Felicity, is looking forward to moving to Secondary School (3 years early) and has been offered a place in the Olympic Wrestling team. Our youngest, Jack has recently qualified as a Neurosurgeon...etc.*

These days, on social media, it's utterly relentless! We need wisdom and perspective. All we are seeing is the highlights. The truth is, you can watch the dullest 90 minutes of football, but when it is condensed into a 60 second highlight reel, it looks really exciting.

We see what others are doing, what they have and how they live and we can think to ourselves, 'Man, they are living the blessed life and for my life to be blessed I should have the same as them.'

Your brother retires early and goes on a six-week cruise and you think to yourself, I should have that too!
Your mate just got a new car – you deserve a new car too.
Our neighbour has a Scandinavian BBQ hut in their back garden – Why don't I have one of those?
(I actually do have one of those in my garden. It's amazing. You should DEFINITELY get one!)

We live in a society that is blighted by this culture of entitlement where everyone believes that they deserve a certain standard of things simply because others have it.

But the truth is, an entitled mindset is the *exact opposite* of living a blessed life and it will rob you of resilience.
Every time.

*****

We should understand that having a resilient life *is* part of our inheritance as followers of Jesus and I have learned that when we have a correct, *Kingdom* attitude towards finances and the 'stuff' we own, the blessed life flows out of that and we will be naturally increasing in resilience.

In the bible, the word 'blessed' is used to speak of many things; divine favour, prosperity and success. Mostly however (especially in the New Testament), it speaks of a condition where you are *deeply secure,*

79

*profoundly content* and *abundantly happy* with your lot and your position in life. For example, at the beginning of Jesus' most famous sermon (the one we know as 'The Sermon on the Mount')[81], He uses the phrase, "Blessed are…" over and over again. This is the translation from the Greek word 'Makarios' which means:

Deeply Secure

Profoundly Content

Abundantly Happy

The point of these 'beatitudes' (as they have become known) is to challenge people's incorrect assumptions about what it means to live a blessed life. Jesus tells us that security, contentment and happiness come from, amongst other things, being poor in spirit, meek, merciful, pure in heart and persecuted.[82]

Yes, you read that correctly.

Blessings can come from persecution.

They can flow out of our troubles.

When we are persecuted for righteousness (right living and right standing before God), happiness, contentment and security follow.

The blessed life is not having a bigger income, a newer car, a fancy home or more 'stuff' than our neighbours. These are nice things sure, and in themselves they are not evil, but the truth is we can have all these and much more and yet still not feel content. They will satisfy for a fleeting instant before the desire for more robs us of happiness. These things do not equate to living a blessed life.

So what is the elusive path that leads to a blessed life?

How can we live in such a way that we are deeply secure, profoundly content and abundantly happy?

How can we exchange our feelings of entitlement and dissatisfaction with feelings of blessing and contentment?

And how can we find a greater resilience through living out God's best life?

There are many clues to these questions throughout scripture that will point us in the right direction.

*****

In the first half of our bible (the bit we call the Old Testament), God gave the people of Israel a set of over six hundred laws - part of which we know as the Ten Commandments - and told them, in essence, if you obey all these laws then you will be blessed, your life will be blessed – in all aspects. You will be blessed individually and as a nation.[83]

You can see how this would be helpful right?
You knew exactly how you stood and what you had to do.
What could possibly go wrong?

God also told them, in essence, if you don't obey these laws then you won't be blessed – in fact you will be cursed – in all aspects of your life – your children, your finances, your crops, your relationships, your nation.
It will all go pear-shaped.[84]
(I'm not sure why the shape of a pear is particularly bad – I quite like pears! The shape of a banana on the other hand…)

*These are the terms of the covenant the Lord commanded Moses to make with the Israelites in Moab*[85]

This is what the Old Covenant was built upon. If you do this, I will do this. If you don't do this…ouch!
It was essentially a two-way contract (known as a suzerain – vassal treaty - a treaty between two unequal parts). There were blessings available from God, but it was conditional.

81

Anyone with a limited knowledge of bible history (or experience of human nature) knows how this all worked out. The nation of Israel rarely managed to fulfil the conditions of the contract and all those curses that God warned about, came to pass.

We can learn from this that simply obeying a set of rules and commandments was not ultimately the way for us to experience God's blessings. Happiness, security and contentment will not be found by simply trying to be a good person.

*****

Let's go back a bit further.
Centuries before the Old Covenant there was an even older covenant!

Many years before God gave the law, through Moses, to the people of Israel, He made a different kind of covenant with a guy called Abram (subsequently called Abraham). Which went something like this...
Because you believe me and believe in me...I am going to bless you. I will make your name great. I am going to make you fruitful in every way. And through you, all the different kinds of people on the earth are going to be blessed. God continued...

*"I will establish my covenant as an everlasting covenant between me and you and your descendants after you for the generations to come, to be your God and the God of your descendants after you."*[86]

God called this agreement with Abraham, an *everlasting* covenant and the great news is that when Jesus came into the earth he was fulfilling this covenant with Abraham (that through Abraham all peoples would be blessed). At the exact same time he was superseding the covenant made with Moses and the nation of Israel (the agreement based on laws and commandments).

In doing this, Jesus ushered in a *brand-new covenant*. A different covenant. A *replacement* covenant to the one made through Moses. Not a two-way contract but a unilateral, unconditional, promissory covenant. A totally different type of contract where one party makes a pledge to another party and takes full responsibility for fulfilling that promise.

Just before he died, Jesus said the following (the words we remember when we take communion):

*"This cup is the <u>new</u> covenant in my blood which is poured out for you"*[87]

Are there blessings in this new covenant?
Yes, but they are blessings not based on what we do or don't do - they are blessings based on faith in God. Trusting in His goodness. Depending on Him for what we need. Believing that He will provide for us.

The blessed life (and most resilient life) is one that is surrendered and submitted to God and the biggest, most important blessing of all is not a blessing we earn by doing something or behaving in a certain way…

*"Blessed are those*
*whose transgressions are forgiven,*
*whose sins are covered.*
*Blessed is the one*
*whose sin the Lord will never count against them."*[88]

This is the fulfilment of God's original covenant with Abraham and is the start of a truly blessed and *resilient* life.

\*\*\*\*\*

If you have faith in God. If you have made the decision to offer your life to Jesus and accept that new covenant for yourself. A covenant that tells us:

*he who had no sin became sin for us, so that in him we might become the righteousness of God.*[89]

He who was sinless, became sin. So that we who had no righteousness could be called righteous.

If you have confessed with your mouth that Jesus is Lord and believed in your heart that God raised Him from the dead,[90] then you have the route to a blessed and resilient life.
Not only that, you have a blessed eternity too!

So how do we take God's idea of a blessed life (complete trust in Him) and turn it into a measure of resilience when we face trouble, particularly in the area of our finances?

In the following chapter we are going to learn some key strategies that will help us develop resilience in our finances and will move us towards being deeply secure, profoundly content and abundantly happy.

# Chapter 8
# An Attitude of Gratitude

*I know what it is to be in need, and I know what it is to have plenty. I have learned the secret of being content in any and every situation, whether well fed or hungry, whether living in plenty or in want.*
*Philippians 4:12*

In this chapter I want to tackle a specific area of life that seems to challenge our resilience again and again – the area of wealth, debt, finances and material possessions. The great news is, the bible (and Jesus in particular) has a great deal of wisdom to share in this area.

In order to become more resilient in our finances, we have to be completely honest with ourselves. Firstly, we should be honest about what our motivation is regarding our finances. Are we always looking for a get-rich-quick scheme or a way to 'keep up with the Jones's'? Do we 'invest' in lottery tickets hoping for those elusive six numbers? Are we waiting for prosperity to fall into our lap so we can show our 'friends' on Facebook that we have truly made it? How do we see our financial resources serving the best and brightest visions of our future?

Perhaps even more difficult than being honest about our desires for the future, we also have to be honest about where we find ourselves right now in our finances. We have to be able to say, 'yeah, I'm really not doing well in this area, in fact I struggle a lot.'

Until we are prepared to consider ourselves 'with sober judgement'[91], we won't ask for the help we need, and we won't put things in place to help us become more resilient.

Often, it's easier to see and confront these things in other people rather than focusing on ourselves and our own shortcomings. Jesus knew this and challenged it up front.

*"How can you say to your brother, 'Let me take the speck out of your eye,' when all the time there is a plank in your own eye?"[92]*

We find it much more comfortable to ignore *our* plank and go for someone else's speck. But the truth is, we will be in a much better position if we examine our own issues first. Get rid of the plank and then you can see clearly. You'll genuinely be able to help others because you can finally see clearly.
Does that remind you of a song?...

*"I can see clearly now the 'plank' has gone.*
*I can see all obstacles in my way"?[93]*

No – not that one!
A different song, by Michael Jackson...

*"I'm starting with the man in the mirror*
*I'm asking him to change his ways*
*No message could have been any clearer*
*If you want to make the world a better place, take a look at yourself and then make the change."[94]*

If you want to make the world a better place,
take a look at yourself and... first remove the enormous plank out of your own eye...and then make the change.
(yes okay, I'll concede his lyrics scan slightly better!)

First be honest about where you at and how you are doing with your finances, then you will be in a position to make better decisions that will contribute towards you having a more resilient life.

*****

Did you know that there are over 2000 references to money, wealth and possessions in the bible? Almost half of all Jesus' parables speak about money, wealth and possessions. There is an abundance of teaching in both the Old and New Testaments that lay out a kingdom approach to our wealth and if we are honest, we know that so much of the trouble we face day to day is often a result of wrong thinking and our own handling of our finances.

First, it's important to understand that money is not evil. The bible tells us that,

*'the love of money is a root of all kinds of evil.'*[95]

Let me say it again: Money itself is not evil. However, our approach to money can make it either beneficial or destructive to us. It all starts with our thinking. We need to be thinking about finances correctly so that money can be a source of help to us, rather than a source of harm. We need to 'not conform to the pattern of this world, but, be transformed by the renewing of [our] mind[96].
Building resilience in our finances starts with new thinking.
A new perspective.

*****

Have you ever played the game Monopoly?
It's a game that, as a child, I played fairly frequently. Honestly, I was pretty rubbish at it.

My older brother thrashed me every time because he was older and smarter than I was.

Now that I'm older and smarter, I play against my own kids.

And... I still get thrashed!

My son, JJ, is a ninja when it comes to all board-games and card-games.

He wins everything -because he's such a dirty cheat!

No he's not really. I'm just bad at games.

We played a few weeks ago and I thought I had him. He had the stations.

Ha ha! The stations are completely pants.

Nobody wins with the stations...

Except JJ did.

Don't ask me how. (I was even the banker)

The trouble with Monopoly is that once you've been around the board a couple of times, you kind of know when you're not going win, and the rest of the game (all three to four hours of it!) you are simply trying to survive until you finally land on Park Lane or Mayfair with a hotel on it (U.K. Monopoly) and it wipes you out for the last time.

You know what I'm talking about, right? You play for hours with that sick feeling in the pit of your stomach. You know you can't win but you keep playing, praying you get sent 'directly to Jail' so you don't have to run the gauntlet of all those houses and hotels.

For many people, life can feel just like that. Just keeping your head above water month to month. That sick feeling of mounting debt. not able to pay imminent bills, no savings in your account when the washing machine dies. You are left with that hollow, helpless feeling that there's no way out.

I question whether it has to be like that. I think life gets like this when we operate according to the rules of this world. The apostle Peter made this observation,

*'Be alert and of sober mind. Your enemy the devil prowls around like a roaring lion looking for someone to devour. Resist him, standing firm in the faith, because you know that the family of believers throughout the world is undergoing the same kind of sufferings.* [97]

This is nowhere *more* true than in our finances. Satan's got this game down to a tee. He's like my son, JJ at monopoly. (Yeah - maybe I shouldn't compare my kids to Satan!)

We can be living our life helpless, feeling like our money is devoured each month. Caught and devoured in a cycle of financial difficulties which we can't seem to break out of.

But if it's true that Jesus has 'overcome the world' and we should 'take heart' then there must be a better way for us live.

In the second half of this chapter I want to provide four principles that have helped me, and countless others turn things around in this difficult area of managing finances.

These four principals are pretty simple, and they are straight from God's word. Fru and I have lived by these principals for two decades and they really work. Trust me – they work. You can stay on the 'Monopoly roundabout' is you like but I would encourage you instead to read on with a soft heart open to something better and potentially life-changing.

*****

## 1. Live within your means.

When I look around at the stress and the chaos that grips this world, particularly in the area of finances and money, I often notice that it's less of an income issue and more of a spending issue. Most of us from

89

time to time, have this thought go through our heads, "if only I could earn more money, my life would be so much better."

There is a spirit of covetousness (wanting to own something that someone else has) in the way our society functions that we, as Christ followers need to transform our minds against. When confronted by a seemingly harmless question about fairness in finance, Jesus made the following statement:

*"Take care, and be on your guard against all covetousness, for one's life does not consist in the abundance of his possessions."*[98]

(In this world that we find ourselves in, I would also add 'experiences' to this value statement. Costly experiences such as holidays, eating out and mani-pedis are no more the substance of our lives than the 'stuff' we own.)

I expect many of us would agree in principle with Jesus' statement here. However, I wonder whether our bank accounts and receipts would tell a different story.

We are bombarded and assaulted with new 'stuff' every day on TV, on billboards, from other people, celebrities, magazines and the internet.
We're all guilty of it.
Something new catches our eye and, even though we can't really afford it, we try and justify it to ourselves.
I need it.
I need this new phone – mine is now 6 months old.
I deserve a break – I'm exhausted.
Everybody else has one.
My life would be so much better if I had it.

Ring any bells?

It takes discipline not to get swept along. We walk through the doors of Costco. And we suddenly and inexplicably get dissatisfied with the size of our current TV.

"Darling, Our TV screen is only 60 inches wide. We really need one that fills the entire wall."

Before walking in the store, I was quite happy with the TV I had until I saw the new Ultra High Definition, curved, OLED, Rich Tone, smart TV! Now of course I realise that my life is terrible and the TV we have is just not good enough!

It's a lie. And we have to actively guard against it.

When our kids were younger, we made up a game that we would regularly play with them. It's a game called 'Where's the lie?' It's a fantastic game and you can play it too. The rules are simple; you see an advert, or a poster, or anything that is trying to sell you something and you ask the question, 'Where's the lie?'

For example, you might see an advertisement where a man splashes a certain brand of aftershave on his face and now he has his pick of all the beautiful women in the world!...Because he smells better.

Really?!

We (society) lap this stuff up and go out and buy what these people are selling, even if it means getting into debt.

We buy things we don't need.

With money we don't have.

To impress people that we don't even like!

(By the way – the answer to the question 'Where's the lie?' is almost always, 'this product will make you a more valuable, happier person and your life will be better if you have it.'

It's great, because once you start seeing the lie in all the adverts you are bombarded with – it makes it much easier to walk away and actually be content with what you have.

*****

In the parable of the sower, Jesus talks about the *deceitfulness* of wealth. Money, wealth, possessions – they are deceitful. They lie to you. They tell you, 'you can't do without me.' They invent this story that you will be a better person, will have more friends, be happier and that your life will be better – if you just upgrade.

It's simply a coveting problem. We desire the life that someone else has and this leads to a debt problem and it's something that we have to kill in us, again and again.

Just the other week, I got annoyed with having to turn the light off in our home office (the room where the kids do their homework). The office is at the far end of our kitchen. It's not a room you ever walk past, it's on the back of the house and you have to walk the entire length of the kitchen to get to it. My children (bless 'em) keep leaving the lights on. In order to turn them off, I have to walk the entire length of the kitchen, into the office, reach round the wall and switch the switch. (I know right – poor me!)

So I had a great idea. I could buy some smart bulbs for the office, and then instead of walking all the way across the kitchen I could simply say, "Alexa, turn off the office lights!" and those pesky lights would switch off all by themselves.
Without the long walk across the kitchen.
How great is that.

So, I ordered the smart light bulbs and they arrived the following day. I opened the box and with a sinking feeling in the pit of my stomach said to myself, 'Adam, you've been duped. You believed the lie. You are a prize Muppet! Why would you think that this was the best solution to the problem? You've just spent a ton of money on light bulbs so that you don't have to walk across a room to turn them off?'

I'm certain it was the Holy Spirit putting me straight. The voice in my head continued, 'Here's an idea – be a better dad and teach your kids to be good stewards of the resources you have (energy - turning off the light) – instead of demonstrating bad stewardship by buying stuff you don't need!'

Unfortunately, the voice wasn't finished yet…
'And…if they don't turn off the light and you have to walk across your kitchen…every single time you do that, say a prayer of thanks to God for providing you with this amazing house with a big kitchen and a room for the kids to do their homework in, with computers and internet and a printer and everything they need. Be grateful for God's blessing!'

I returned the smart bulbs to Amazon.

Let's not buy into this world's pattern. Let's stop putting pressure on our parents and our spouses to give us things it's not our season to have.

\*\*\*\*\*

A quick word for young people – your parents have worked decades to get to the position they are in with the possessions they have…don't be under the mistaken impression that you should have the same things or the same life. It's simply not your season yet.

*I know what it is to be in need, and I know what it is to have plenty. I have learned the secret of being content in any and every situation, whether well fed or hungry, whether living in plenty or in want. I can do all this through him who gives me strength.*[99]

Live within your means. Be content. Find the lie in the pressure to own more stuff – it doesn't make you happier. If anything, it actually feeds your discontentment.

Do you need to buy that Starbucks coffee every day? – Two coffees a day. Five times a week works out to about £1500 per year. Do you need to upgrade your phone? Do you need another pair of shoes that will sit in your wardrobe next to the other five, ten, twenty pairs? Do you need executive membership of that golf club? Just so you can feel 'important' as you slice another shot into the trees? A new handbag? That you'll then want to buy more stuff to fill.

Please understand, I'm not saying become a miser. I'm not saying that God wants you to live with lack or poverty. Just the opposite in fact. I'm simply saying; look at what is coming in, save some, give some away, look at what is left and don't spend more than that.

Don't be driven by a covetous eye. Be driven by a Godly vision. A vision that sees a future that is better than the past or the present. A vision that enables you to make the hard decisions. To go without right now, so that you can live without the stress of debt. To go without today so that your tomorrow can be better.

When you see something that attracts your eye – ask yourself – 'where's the lie?' Can I live without it? If you do need it, save up for it. Live within your means. This is a sure way to bring about an increased measure of resilience in your life.

*****

2. **Integrity in your finances.**

This is the second principle to help build resilience in your finances. Having integrity in your life is nowhere more important than in your finances and your financial dealings.

Integrity is a great word. We all kind of know what it means to have integrity right? At the root of this concept is the word 'integer'. Maybe you recall this concept from your maths lessons at school. An integer is a whole number. And that's what it means to have integrity.
To be whole.
To not have sections or compartments in your life.
To not be two-faced or double-minded.
To be the same person, with the same values in every situation.

To have integrity in your finances, means that you live your life doing what you know is right, in every circumstance, whether someone is looking or not.

Now I'm sure that most of us are not going to go out and rob a bank, mug someone or break into someone's home to steal stuff. But maybe there are some areas where perhaps we are not living with the integrity we should.

Did you know that, in the UK, two hundred million pounds worth of stuff is stolen every year from workplaces. Perhaps you don't think that taking a pen or a notebook or paperclips from your workplace office is stealing.

Maybe you don't think that downloading a film or a piece of music from the internet without paying for it does anybody any harm. Downloading a film to watch is not going to bankrupt Universal Pictures. However, I do believe that this approach harms you.

As Christians, we want to live in the blessing of God, in *all* areas of our lives. In order for God to bless us – and by blessing us I mean to hear those words 'Well done good and faithful servant. You have been faithful in small things, I can trust you now with bigger things.'[100] - we have to be trustworthy stewards with the resources He has given us. This is an important kingdom principle. When we have integrity in the small things – we can be entrusted with more. That is what being blessed ultimately means.

We need to be faithful in all things, including the small things. It doesn't take faith to steal pens from work, download music or movies, cheat a little on your tax returns or walk out of a store knowing they have given you more change than you should have received. It takes faith to say to God, 'You alone are my provider so I'm going to trust that you will provide everything I need and if I can't afford to buy that film I really want to watch  - then I'm going to wait to watch it until I can afford it or it comes on TV.'
Well done – good and faithful servant.

*****

Again – this is an area we need to be vigilant in. Just this week there was a music track I needed for use in a church service. I was tempted to just go on to YouTube – and rip (download) the track. This is not a piece of music that I'm ever going to want to listen to again. I just needed it for the service.

That small voice inside my head said, 'Ninety-nine pence Adam? You don't trust God to provide ninety-nine pence to buy this track legitimately? You don't even have the faith for that?!' (you've got to love the Holy Spirit)
What was I thinking?

This is not about whether or not I'm going to listen to the track a hundred times or never. You do the right thing simply because it's the right thing.

In *every* situation.

That's what integrity is.

It's not about the amount – it's about the principle. Do you remember the widow who put two small coins in the temple offering? Jesus explained that she has put more in than all the others who were putting in large amounts.[101] If Jesus noticed and valued two small copper coins which practically made no difference, he will certainly notice 99 pence, a paper clip or an extra five minutes on the end of your lunchbreak!

The truth is, it is definitely in the small acts, when no one is looking, that we make or break our integrity.

I love the account of Zacchaeus. He was a tax collector – a mobster really – he ripped people off under the guise of collecting taxes. He encountered Jesus one day and it completely changed his thinking.

*"Look, Lord! Here and now I give half of my possessions to the poor, and if I have cheated anybody out of anything, I will pay back four times the amount."*
*Jesus said to him, "Today salvation has come to this house,"[102]*

Live with integrity in your finances. Pay your debts. Don't always try and get the upper hand in a transaction. Pay for what you need. Don't 'borrow' someone else's Netflix account.

Having integrity attracts God's blessing and builds a healthy resilience in your life and particularly in your finances.

\*\*\*\*\*

### 3. Live generously

The third principle that will promote resilience in your life is generosity.

Let me tell you something about money and wealth that may well be new information. It doesn't change who you are. Having it or not having it doesn't change you. If you are not generous when you don't have it. You won't be generous when you do have it.

How many times have I heard the phrase, 'If I just had a little more money, I could afford to be generous'?

This is not how it works. Having more money has never made a person generous. Money is actually an amplifier. It simply amplifies whatever character you already have.

I remember one of my children learning to play the violin.

It was excruciating!

Every morning (for many months) they would pick up the instrument and play scales and simple tunes and it sounded like a pack of cats being strangled!

It was bad enough hearing it from another room in our home.

Now if I decided to set up a microphone next to the violin and put the sound through a one thousand-watt P.A system, it's not going to sound better.

It's actually going to sound a thousand times worse right?

Money works in the same way. It is an amplifier. It will only intensify what it already there.

A stingy person who uses the excuse of having no money for their stinginess is, at best, misinformed and at worst – a liar.

However, if I don't have a lot but I train myself to be generous, when more comes along – I'll still be generous – but now I am able to be generous with more. (when our daughter sounds good on the violin, in say - twenty to thirty years, I will be happy to mic her up!)

*****

So how do I begin to be generous with what I have?

*All the believers were one in heart and mind. No one claimed that any of their possessions was their own, but they shared everything they had*[103]

There is something pretty radical going on here.

Eliza is our youngest daughter. She recently learned the word that all children learn at quite a young age – 'Mine!'.

As we get older, we don't say it out loud anymore, but we still think it. This attitude is the source of all kinds of envy and anxiety and greed. This attitude is often the foundation of all kinds of crimes, wars, murders and civil unrest.

However, here was the early church's approach:
It's not my stuff.
It's not your stuff.
It's not our stuff.
It's not the leader's stuff.
Whose stuff is it?
It's God's stuff.

Letting go of ownership and the whole 'mine!' attitude to living is the start of experiencing a real freedom in our life.

We need to have the perspective of a steward rather than an owner. God gives us good things, but we are not on this earth to hoard and grow our pile. God gives to us for us to give to others. He blesses us so that we can be a blessing.
This is a kingdom principle that we find throughout scripture. See if you can spot the deliberate errors in the following bible passages:

*The Lord had said to Abram...'I will make you into a great nation, and I will bless you; I will make your name great... and you can keep all those lovely blessings for yourself and have a great life!."*

Did you spot it? I really hope you did.
God actually says,

*"and all peoples on earth will be blessed through you."*[104]

The point of the blessing was for it to pour out through Abram to the rest of mankind.
How about this one:

*And God is able to bless you abundantly, so that in all things at all times, having all that you need...you will finally be able to keep up with your neighbours.*

Not quite no.
What it actually says is:

*And God is able to bless you abundantly, so that in all things at all times, having all that you need you will abound in every good work.*[105]

God blesses abundantly. Why? So that we can abound in *every good work*.
The blessing comes in.
The blessing goes through us, out to others.
One more:

*Now he who supplies seed to the sower and bread for food will also supply and increase your store of seed and will enlarge the harvest of your righteousness. You will be enriched in every way so that...you can eat lots, buy all the gadgets you want and spoil your kids.*

Not so much.

What Paul actually writes is:

*You will be enriched in every way so that you can be generous on every occasion, and through us your generosity will result in thanksgiving to God.[106]*

Do I believe that God sends his blessing on us – no doubt. But we have to remind ourselves continually that the blessings are a seed – not a harvest for consumption. We are not containers of God's blessing, we are conduits.

\*\*\*\*\*

**We are conduits, not containers of God's blessing.**

It comes in – it goes out. As it goes out, more comes in. The more we send out, the more he blesses us. In fact, the more we give out, He not only fills the space, He increases our capacity.

*"Give and it will be given to you, A good measure, pressed down, shaken together and running over, will be poured into your lap. For with the measure you use, it will be measured to you."[107]*

*The world of the generous gets larger and larger. The world of the stingy gets smaller and smaller.[108]*

Living a life that truly understands how God's blessings work will bring such a freedom. Moving away from a 'mine' attitude to a generous lifestyle is one of the surest ways to build resilience in your finances.

\*\*\*\*\*

### 4. Put God First

I've already written a little about trusting God in all things, but I want to end this chapter by talking about a specific action we can take that God has ordained as a way that demonstrates our trust in him.

It's the principle of Firstfruits. The idea of this principle is that we give to God the first and best of what comes in. In ancient times this would mean at harvest time, bringing to the temple a portion of your harvest, specifically the first amount that you bring in. In the lambing season, it would mean bringing the first animals born from your flock.

The idea being that when you say to God, 'here is the first portion', you are, in effect saying, 'I totally trust you to bless the rest and provide all I need.'

*Honor the Lord with your wealth,*
*with the firstfruits of all your crops;*
*then your barns will be filled to overflowing,*
*and your vats will brim over with new wine.*[109]

We see this Firstfruits principle encouraged throughout scripture (both Old and New Testament) and you may even put this principle into practice today without knowing it.

Maybe you have a quiet time with God at the beginning of each day – I've found that the rest of the day seems to be just that bit more balanced when I do this.

Every week, believers all over the world come together to serve and praise God in church on Sundays. In effect, giving the first day of the week to God.

At the beginning of each year, in our family and I know in many other church families, we fast for the first week. This is simply saying, 'Here is the first of my year God. I trust you with my whole year.'

And each month when my wages come into my bank account. I set aside the first portion to come straight out of my account into the church I attend and lead. I give God the Firstfruits, and say 'I trust you God to keep me and my family with the rest.'

In the way I give I like to take my cue from the apostle Paul's teaching that giving should be regular and disciplined.[110]

This doesn't stop me being spontaneous. Giving as and when I see a need or am prompted by the Holy Spirit to do so.
But there is wisdom in planned, regular and disciplined giving. Sporadic giving with no plan will probably mean I am not treating giving as an integral part of my worshipping life.

As I learn to trust God in this way, I have found it has an effect on *every* area of my life. I am simply more resilient because I lean on Him. I magnify Him. And what I have discovered is that He is faithful.
Always.
He cannot be anything else.

*****

How much should I give?
My answer would start with the Old Testament standard (that's where we get the word tithe – which simply means ten percent) and build on that as God blesses you. There's this amazing passage in the book of Malachi that, a number of years ago, significantly altered mine and my family's life.

*"Will a mere mortal rob God? Yet you rob me.*
*"But you ask, 'How are we robbing you?'*
*"In tithes and offerings. You are under a curse—your whole nation—because you are robbing me. Bring the whole tithe into the storehouse, that there may be food in my house. Test me in this," says the Lord Almighty, "and see if I will not throw*

*open the floodgates of heaven and pour out so much blessing that there will not be room enough to store it. I will prevent pests from devouring your crops, and the vines in your fields will not drop their fruit before it is ripe," says the Lord Almighty. "Then all the nations will call you blessed, for yours will be a delightful land," says the Lord Almighty.[111]*

Becoming disciplined in this area of giving was arguably the single largest tangible factor in gaining resilience in my finances and in many ways, my whole life.

I really believe that obedience in this area this will lead to a blessed life.

I love those words we just read from Malachi. 'Test me in this…'. I'm pretty sure that this is the only circumstance in scripture where God specifically asks us to test him. I would encourage you to take God up on this promise. Why don't you 'test' this act of disciplined, regular giving and see if this really works.

I'm confident that when we put these 4 principles in place – Living within our means, living with integrity, living generously and putting God first, we will ultimately arrive at a place of greater resilience, especially in our finances but probably in many other areas too.

Perhaps it's time to start with the Man (or woman) in the Mirror and begin to make some changes.

Today.

# Chapter 9
# Unity begins with 'U'

*And over all these virtues put on love,*
*which binds them all together in perfect unity.*
*Colossians 4:13*

I have been present and 'involved' (as involved as the father can be) at the birth of four of my kids. I loved the beautiful and unique experience of seeing new life come into this world, although if I'm honest, there were moments when I was less than helpful to my wife. I actually passed out a couple of times during the last two deliveries. Now before you start judging, I only became light-headed because the birthing room was really hot, and I hadn't eaten enough. That's my excuse and I'm sticking to it!

Yep – I sound like the kind of man you need in a time of crisis, right?

New-born babies are amazing, and they are a wonder to look at and hold. I've noticed that one of the first things that a lot of people do when confronted with a new baby is to immediately compare him or her to someone else. They feel the need to attach some kind of label – straightaway.

'Oh - she looks just like you.'

'She has her mum's eyes.'

'Her jaw line is just like her great grandfathers.'

'Her feet are the spitting image of her brothers.'

Handing out labels and putting people in distinct boxes is something we all feel the need to do. It's somehow satisfying and, dare I say it, 'neater' to be able to define people in a specific and familiar way. And yet we know labels can be so destructive – they create separation and division. Many of the conflicts and wars throughout history have come about when one group of people define themselves in a different way to another group.

Whether the definition is to do with race, social status, gender or skin-colour, we know that division between people is generally not a good thing but often we just can't seem to help ourselves from putting labels on people. That said, we should keep on working towards this generation getting the ball further down the field than ever before.

And it is sad to admit it but the church, historically, hasn't been guilt-free in this regard. There have been labels created for those inside the church by those outside, and vice versa. There have even been labels *within* the Church that have caused much division and created the many Christian denominations that we now live with.

One group of people focus on Baptism, but another focuses on the Holy Spirit. One group emphasises biblical teaching, another spotlights worship. There are even labels created inside individual churches that create offense and separation.

'I like loud contemporary music.'

'I like softer, more traditional worship.'

'I like a pipe organ.'

I like soft chairs.'

'I prefer hard, uncomfortable pews.' (Actually, nobody says that.)

One group of people find a particular interpretation of scripture and build walls of doctrine around it. Some folk are included, and some are excluded. Some inside, others outside. And then each person or group seeks to defend their position by trying to prove why they are right and everyone else is wrong. This has caused a huge amount of division and animosity and I think deep down we all know it's just not the way it's supposed to be. So often the root of division is simply pride. We get prideful about the way we see ourselves and compare ourselves to others and regard them unfavourably.

Division creates animosity, dysfunction and emotional ill-health.
Unity creates understanding, well-being and *resilience*.

*****

Being in healthy relationship with other people helps you progress further in life. Unity promotes increased emotional health, helping propel you through those challenges and troubles that life throws your way.

Did you know that Jesus himself prayed about this? He knew all about human nature as well as anyone and He knew that division and disunity was a potential trap that his disciples could easily fall into. So, he prayed to God against it.

*'My prayer is not for them alone*

(not just his disciples who were with him there and then).

*I pray also for those who will believe in me through their message,* (that includes us too!) *that all of them may be one, Father, just as you are in me and I am in you. May they also be in us so that the world may believe that you have sent me. I have given them the glory that you gave me, that they may be one as we are one – I in them and you in me – so that they may be brought to complete unity. Then the world will know that you sent me and have loved them even as you have loved me.'*[112]

Jesus wanted his followers to be 'one'. To be united. He wanted us to experience the same unity with each other that Jesus and the Father experienced. He wanted our relationships with each other to be *that* deep.
*That* connected.
*That* resilient!

*****

Jesus was so convinced of this that he made it his final prayer before his arrest. In essence, he is saying, "Father – please give them what they need to that they can have unity". He knew it wouldn't happen naturally. He knew it needed divine intervention. He knew that the Enemy's game plan was destruction. He said it himself, 'The enemy (the devil) comes to steal, kill and destroy;'[113]

And the devil's strategy for accomplishing that game plan is division.

And his main tactic to accomplish this strategy?

Pride.

*God opposes the proud*[114] because pride gets in the way of unity.

It short-circuits resilience.

Pride causes us to think too highly of ourselves and our own opinions and our own way of doing things and it creates separation between us and those who perhaps disagree with us. This is an area that we all struggle with. We all hate to be wrong. If I have a disagreement with Fru, my wife, I want to be right. Even when I suspect I'm wrong, I *especially* want to be right then. Do you know anyone like that? I think most of us have a little (or perhaps more than a little) of that in us.

So, Jesus prayed to his father and asked for intervention in order that there might be unity in His people.

The great news is, the Father answered this prayer. What would it take for us to be one? To have that connected, resilient relationship that Jesus prayed about?

It would take a miracle.

And that miracle occurred a few weeks later just as the Church was about to be birthed.

*****

We find this miracle - this answered prayer - in the book of Acts and in the same passage we can also see the blueprint for how we, who would call ourselves as 'followers of Jesus Christ', should behave towards one another.

It's the day of Pentecost – 50 days after Passover and 50 days since Jesus has resurrected. Jesus had told his followers to wait in Jerusalem for the Holy Spirit to come and that's what they have been doing.

Throughout the gospels, we read how Jesus' disciples were a diverse bunch of guys that He chose at the start of his earthly ministry.
He didn't choose apprentices who were similar in nature to himself or each other.
They didn't have lots in common.
They weren't all from the same social class.
They wouldn't naturally hang out together.

He chose rough and ready fishermen, tradesmen, a despised tax collector, a zealot. Some of them were outspoken, others more reserved. There were even women who were part of this close group (unheard of in this historical context).
We also know from the gospel text that they weren't especially united.
Or particularly resilient. (at least initially)
They had arguments, they fell out, they wanted to elevate themselves over each other.

Earlier in his ministry, Jesus had said

*'A house divided against itself cannot stand'.*[115]

Something had to change.
Unity was a crucial requirement for Jesus' plan for His Church.

At the beginning of the narrative in Acts chapter two, the believers are doing what Jesus had instructed; they are waiting in Jerusalem and are 'all together in one place' when the Holy Spirit comes on them. There are various accompanying supernatural signs; a noise that sounds like a violent wind, a filling of the Holy Spirit, tongues of fire appearing above their heads and they begin speaking in other languages 'as the Spirit enabled them'.[116]

The narrative immediately moves from inside the upper room where the believers are 'together', to outside in Jerusalem where the writer (Dr. Luke) starts to label all the various peoples and nationalities who are there:

*Parthians, Medes, Elamites, residents of Mesopotamia, Judea and Cappadocia, Pontus and Asia, Phrygia and Pamphylia, Egypt, Libya, Cyrene, visitors from Rome, Cretans and Arabs.*[117]

All this potential for division and separation. In fact, we know that this society was built upon division. The Jewish people were very much into dividing people into categories based on nationality and religion – Jews and non-Jews (Gentiles). The Romans were very much into dividing people into status - rich, poor, slave and freeman. We also know that at this time and throughout history there was huge gender dysfunction – Women and girls were mostly considered second class citizens and not entitled to the same rights and privileges as men.

Unfortunately, many of these dividing issues we still face in some measure today.
Across the world, the issue of racism is still rearing its ugly head. Even as I write this chapter, there are massive protests happening in many cities and countries throughout the world in support of the 'Black Lives Matter' movement, after police in Minneapolis killed George Floyd.

Status is also still hugely divisive – where do you live? What do you wear? Where do you work? How do you speak? How much do you earn?

110

We literally can't seem to help ourselves – we look at people and immediately make a judgement about them – Do they fit in? Are they one of us?

The apostle Paul spoke right into this when he was talking to the church in Galatia. He wants to let them know that these differences are not elements that should separate us. He states,

*So in Christ Jesus you are all children of God through faith… There is neither Jew nor Gentile, neither slave nor free, nor is there male and female, for you are all one in Christ Jesus.*[118]

He's covering it all there – race and nationality should no longer divide us.
Our status or wealth shouldn't divide us.
Our gender shouldn't divide us
We are all ONE – united in Christ Jesus.

*****

Back to Jerusalem. We have all these nationalities gathered together for the Passover celebration and right into this jumble of diverse people, out of the upper room come the disciples and (more importantly) The Holy Spirit.
This is the miracle.
This is the answer to the prayer that Jesus made a few weeks earlier.
Not just for his followers then, but for anyone throughout history who would become his disciple.
The world would never be the same again.

As we continue reading through this passage at the start of the book of Acts, we discover that thousands of lives were changed on this day as a result of the Holy Spirit. One of the biggest changes was Jesus' follower's capacity for Unity.

111

At the end of this narrative - after it tells us that three thousand became believers – we read the following,

*They devoted themselves to the apostles' teaching and to fellowship, to the breaking of bread and to prayer. Everyone was filled with awe at the many wonders and signs performed by the apostles. All the believers were together and had everything in common. They sold property and possessions to give to anyone who had need. Every day they continued to meet together in the temple courts. They broke bread in their homes and ate together with glad and sincere hearts, praising God and enjoying the favour of all the people. And the Lord added to their number daily those who were being saved.[119]*

That's the miracle.
It's the blueprint for the church.
Unity.
Which is a bedrock for resilience.

*****

There is an old proverb, often quoted; *He travels fastest who travels alone.* But there is a second part to this saying that is usually left out but is vitally important; *He travels furthest who travels with others.*

The disciples are about to go on an incredible journey. A journey that would reach across millennia. A journey to take the good news of Jesus in ever-widening circles, from 'Jerusalem, and in all Judea and Samaria, and to the ends of the earth.'[120]
This journey wasn't about speed. It wasn't about getting the message out as fast as possible. It was a journey that would need endurance and resilience. They were the pioneers of a movement that would ultimately see tremendous growth. They are going to need to rely on each other, support one other, trust one other. Some of them will be imprisoned together and even be tortured and martyred together. All for the sake of the mission they've been given.

The coming of the Holy Spirit on the day of Pentecost gave these Jesus-followers (and gives us too) the possibility of a divine connection – not only to God but to each other. It turns disconnected and diverse people into a united, unified entity. This is what the Church was always meant to be.

Resilient.

A close family.

A united body. Not united with gritted teeth but actually enjoying our God-given differences.

Families might disagree, they might fall out sometimes, they might have different opinions, but they are...family.

*****

Before our youngest, Eliza was born, our other kids (who were significantly older) were naturally cautious about what it would mean to have another sibling (and a baby). They were happy of course, but there was a reservation about how it would affect our home and our family as it was. But as soon as Eliza arrived, all those concerns and apprehensions just didn't seem important anymore.

Was Eliza different?

Yes – she was a baby!

Did she bring a new dynamic into our home and family?

Yes! Did she cry a lot? And poop a lot? And stop us sleeping?

Yes. Yes. Yes!.

But that is not as important as the fact that she was part of our family. She belonged with us. We are a family and we are united! And we are stronger and more resilient, together.

*****

As well as being a family, The Church is also described as a body. A body made up of different parts that can only function effectively when it's connected to the whole. There is no more important parts or less important parts. Everyone is needed and everyone is connected. The Holy Spirit intentionally gives us different gifts that are there to complement one another. It doesn't make us all the same, but it does make us a body and it does make us united.

*****

As well as being a family and a body, The Church is also described as a temple.[121] The crucial element of this image being that we are bricks built on the foundation that is Jesus Christ. He is our cornerstone and the rest of us are built in line with Him.

A cornerstone is one of the first bricks or stones that you would lay when erecting a new building. All of the other elements of the building are then placed so that they are level and in-line to that stone.
And this is what brings our unity – being aligned to Jesus.
If every brick was placed without reference to a set 'standard' then the building won't be level. It would look like a complete mess and would ultimately lose its strength.

The same is true for us. We can't all align to ourselves, creating our own standard, moral judgements or even gospel and think it's all going to work out. We can't even align ourselves to the bricks (people) around us – we will simply build cliques and bring division into the church.

When *all* the bricks are arranged in line with the cornerstone then they *automatically* align to all the other bricks. When we live our life according to the pattern that Jesus gave, we become aligned to Him and unity follows.

Resilience is born of out of unity and community. We were never created to move through life in isolation. Just as God the Father exists in perfect community with Jesus the Son and The Holy Spirit, we were created (in His image) to exist in community with God and with people around us.

We draw strength and resilience from leaning on others when the troubles of this world face us.

(Even as I'm writing this, I'm imagining Fru, my wife, laughing hysterically at my hypocritical words. I know this is an area that I haven't been particularly great at in the past. I am definitely a work in progress when it comes to learning to lean on others for support but I'm trying and I really believe it's a better way!)

As well as drawing strength when we lean on others, we also draw strength and resilience from being someone who others can lean on when they are facing difficult seasons.
Community is a two-way street that benefits all parties.

If we want to live resilient lives then living in community with others is not an optional extra, it's an essential. It's the pattern that God intended, and He even promises blessings when we do it:

*How good and pleasant it is*
*when God's people live together in unity!*
*2 It is like precious oil poured on the head,*
*running down on the beard,*
*running down on Aaron's beard,*
*down on the collar of his robe.*
*3 It is as if the dew of Hermon*
*were falling on Mount Zion.*
*For there the Lord bestows his blessing,*
*even life for evermore.*[122]

115

Let me say it again for emphasis: Living our lives in community with others, united in purpose and thought, trusting and leaning on each other with God at the centre releases the blessing of God over our lives *and* increases our resilience. It multiplies our ability to handle the storms of life and gives meaning to our existence.

Recent scientific studies have demonstrated clear links between increased social isolation and a reduction in life expectancy. In other words, being an active member of a thriving community or group helps you live longer!

*****

So, what can we practically do to build our resilience inside a community?

1. Find a spiritual home with a church family.

This will provide opportunities for you to worship and participate with other people. Don't just belong to a congregation, actively involve yourself within it. Find a ministry where you can use your talents and passions to serve others.

2. Join a midweek group of people you can relate to (Small Group, Life Group, Home Group, etc.)

The power of the small group is to know people intimately and be known by them — warts and all! This takes time and investment. Meet with them as often as you are able and as trust grows and relationships deepen, share your life with them as much as you are willing. From my own experience, whenever trials and difficulties have hit my own life, it's been my Small Group that has rallied around and been the greatest source of help to me. Be real and honest about your struggles. Be willing to support others in their struggles. Eat together sometimes, laugh together a lot, cry together occasionally, talk together, maybe sing together, study together, serve together. When you are together, Jesus is there with you.

*'if two of you on earth agree about anything they ask for, it will be done for them by my father in heaven. For where two or three gather in my name, there I am with them.'*[123]

3. Look for ways to support and encourage the people around you

As paradoxical as it sounds, one of the most effective ways of building personal resilience is to help other people. When we sacrificially give of ourselves to others, there is a divine replenishment that takes place inside us. Again, there are many scientific studies that show that living for something outside of yourself is an extremely healthy position to take and has even shown to be an effective remedy against depression and anxiety.

*Therefore encourage one another and build each other up, just as in fact you are doing.*[124]

4. Ask for help and support from others when you need it

As well as giving support to others, we need to be people who are not too prideful to ask for help when it's needed. Asking for help from someone is, in many ways, even more effective at building relationships than offering help. I remember reading a study about how the simple act of going to a neighbour to borrow something strengthens society and builds community. Giving someone an opportunity to help you when you are in need will generate value in their own lives and create resilience in both of you.

5. Pray for the people around you regularly

It's truly amazing how much closer you get to people by simply praying for them. I have found (even with people I don't naturally like!) that when I pray for them, it opens a window of understanding and empathy inside me that wasn't evident previously. It's good to make a list of the people you are praying for and keep regular, intentional times where you speak to God about them. Asking Him to show you what to pray for and how you can be a support to them practically.

*Rejoice always, pray continually, give thanks in all circumstances; for this is God's will for you in Christ Jesus.*[125]

\*\*\*\*\*

As we begin to open our lives to others more and more, perhaps we will begin to see each other as a family.

Do we have to agree about everything?  Of course not! I don't know what your family is like but mine certainly doesn't do that.

Do we all need to be the same? No way - that would be hideous! A church or group filled with people just like any one of us would be a disaster (and ultimately a lie)!

We need unity, not uniformity.

Unity is where differences are celebrated, and we recognise the strength that is inherent in each of us bringing who we are (warts and all) to the table. Paul spoke extensively about the value of our differences in his letter to the Corinthian church.

*Just as a body, though one, has many parts, but all its many parts form one body, so it is with Christ. For we were all baptized by one Spirit so as to form one body— whether Jews or Gentiles, slave or free —and we were all given the one Spirit to drink. Even so the body is not made up of one part but of many.*[126]

Just like the early church, we are called to be a fellowship. I've heard it described as fellows on the same ship! I recently saw a picture of a sinking boat. At one end of the boat there was a group of people bailing furiously and at the other end there's two guys just sitting there. One of the guys turns to the other and says, "Thank God that hole is not in our end of the boat!"
This is a telling picture of division in the church.
If a house is divided against itself can't stand.[127]

If we look around us and see people in our community struggling, and we think it doesn't affect us, we are misunderstanding what it is to be in unity. When one suffers – we all suffer[128] – that's the nature of a body and a family.

The benefits of building unity are not just the blessing and resilience that is increased in us. Remember Jesus' prayer from the beginning of this chapter?

*Then the world will know that you sent me and have loved them even as you have loved me.[129]*

It's in our unity as The Church that the whole world will understand the true gospel of Jesus.

Can we be a people where the Holy Spirit rules?
Where an attitude of unity prevails?
Where a heart of encouragement is evident not only to those inside the church but to those we are trying to reach too?

If the Church can live in unity, then I am convinced that the whole world will be transformed by our message and we will experience a measure of resilience that is unshakable.

# Chapter 10
# The Serving Paradox

*It is absolutely clear that God has called you to a free life. Just make sure that you don't use this freedom as an excuse to do whatever you want to do and destroy your freedom. Rather, use your freedom to serve one another in love; that's how freedom grows.*

*Galatians 5:13 (The Message Bible)*

When we think about the word 'resilience', and the type of people who exhibit this trait in their lives, I imagine that for many of us it might conjure up an image of people in positions of power, business executives, rulers, alpha types, athletes and leaders with a high level of self-discipline. Outwardly, these kinds of people always seem to have it together. They exude a self-confidence and an assertiveness that others are drawn to. That's generally what makes them successful in their field.

However, true resilience is not an outward personality trait, it's an internal strength that is only really evident when the proverbial 'mess' hits the fan. Resilience is borne out of character and a sense of self-worth. If we feel 'free' in our lives, if we truly understand the freedom that Jesus has paid for and called us to live in, then true resilience will flow out of that. Whenever the troubles of life hit us, our sense of freedom will act like a layer of armour that prevents us buckling under the pressure and will keep us moving forward.

I really love the paradox that Paul uses to explain the connection between freedom and serving that we read in the scripture at the top of this chapter;

*'use your freedom to serve one another in love; that's how freedom grows.'*[130]

The more we become like a servant, the more freedom we experience.

Our freedom grows when we serve one another in love.

Now it's true that the bible has a lot to say about 'love'.

And 'serving'.

And, come to think about it, it also has plenty to say about 'one another'!

But rather than focus on biblical passages that describe love and service as abstract concepts, I want to focus on a specific time and event, described in the bible, that I think gives us a true understanding of God's capacity for love, service and freedom, and also the capacity for these things He has placed within us.

*****

This moment takes place towards the end of Jesus' three years of ministry, on the evening before his death. Jesus has returned to Jerusalem from Bethany and He and his disciples have checked into a room to spend the evening celebrating the Passover Feast and hanging out together. It's clear that Jesus has a number of important things He needs to tell them.

We pick up the event during the meal. Jesus has eaten the Passover meal with them and established the sacrament of Communion as an important, ongoing practice. Jesus begins talking to the disciples and one of those closest to him will record what takes place. All four of the gospels record the event we know as the Last Supper, but we are going to specifically look at John's (arguably the closest disciple to Jesus) description of it.

We find this moment in the John's gospel, chapters thirteen through seventeen. These are five monumental chapters loaded with the promises of the Lord for those he loved. He speaks at length about the importance of unity (see the previous chapter of this book), the coming of the Holy Spirit as an advocate for His people, his impending death and resurrection, faith, eternity and the troubles his followers would face. This is the final legacy of Jesus to his own and it's truly amazing how he begins this important moment.

*It was just before the Passover Festival. Jesus knew that the hour had come for him to leave this world and go to the Father. Having loved his own who were in the world, he loved them to the end.*[131]

This sets up the whole scene. Jesus is only too aware of what's about to take place. Everything that follows later that evening, and in the days to come, are a practical outworking of his love for humanity. This short introduction sets out the context for God's plan for salvation and his ultimate motivation for his sacrifice. And John's description of Jesus' actions and words over these next five chapters is like a 'song of God' expressing his love for His own. When John writes that He loved them 'to the end', he is describing a love that is complete, to the max, to infinity and beyond, immeasurable and inconceivable.

John continues...

*Jesus knew that the Father had put all things under his power, and that he had come from God and was returning to God; so he got up from the meal, took off his outer clothing, and wrapped a towel around his waist. After that, he poured water into a basin and began to wash his disciples' feet, drying them with the towel that was wrapped around him.*
*He came to Simon Peter, who said to him, "Lord, are you going to wash my feet?"*
*Jesus replied, "You do not realize now what I am doing, but later you will understand."*
*"No," said Peter, "you shall never wash my feet."*
*Jesus answered, "Unless I wash you, you have no part with me."*
*"Then, Lord," Simon Peter replied, "not just my feet but my hands and my head as well!"*

*Jesus answered, "Those who have had a bath need only to wash their feet; their whole body is clean. And you are clean, though not every one of you." For he knew who was going to betray him, and that was why he said not every one was clean. When he had finished washing their feet, he put on his clothes and returned to his place. "Do you understand what I have done for you?" he asked them. "You call me 'Teacher' and 'Lord,' and rightly so, for that is what I am. Now that I, your Lord and Teacher, have washed your feet, you also should wash one another's feet. I have set you an example that you should do as I have done for you. Very truly I tell you, no servant is greater than his master, nor is a messenger greater than the one who sent him. Now that you know these things, you will be blessed if you do them.* [132]*

First of all, let's provide some context to this scene.

As you walk up to a stone, whitewashed home in first century Palestine, you would notice a pot of water either just outside or just inside the front entrance. Before you entered the home, you would be expected to remove your sandals and wash your feet from all the dust and grime you might have picked up from the road. In more wealthy homes, it would be the job of the lowest slave in the household to do this for you. This was a necessary task, though I imagine, not particularly enjoyable. These days it might be equivalent of putting the rubbish out, emptying the dishwasher, cleaning the bathrooms or washing the dishes after every meal. (I only mention these specific chores because in my home, these are the ways that my adorable kids lovingly serve each other. They don't know how good they have it! If we lived in Jesus time, they could have been chief foot-washer!)

As you walked further into this first century home, you might notice a table. Not a dining table with chairs around it that you would find in today's homes, but a low table, close to the floor. In this culture, you wouldn't usually eat a meal like Passover sat up at a table. You would be reclining next to your food, most likely on a cushion on the floor. Your head would be right next to someone's feet. Hence the importance of cleaning between your toes as you come into the home.

In the passage we are looking at, it appears that possibly the disciples hadn't cleaned their feet before coming to the table which means they were all laying there with grimy feet just inches from the head of the person next to them. Maybe there was no slave to help them with this menial task, or poor planning on the part of one of the disciples:


PETER: "Hey Bartholemew! You forgot the foot water, you numpty!"
BARTHOLEMEW (looking slightly hurt): "Well at least he didn't call me Satan!"
PETER (squaring up): "You talkin' to me? You talkin' to me?!"
(Jesus quietly fills a bowl stage right)


Possibly this lack of foot-washing slave led to the argument they were having, about which of them was the greatest! (you can read this in Luke's record of this Passover meal – chapter 22)


How would you feel if you were Jesus in this moment? The disciples have effectively acknowledged that you are the Messiah, or at the very least a very great prophet or Rabbi, and yet here they are arguing about which of themselves was the greatest.
This is your 'going away party'.
You should be holding the place of honour.
You should be exalted.
But instead, your closest friends are arguing about how great *they* are.
And they've got stinky feet!


I'm pretty sure I wouldn't handle it well. When I see people being self-centered, I want to lay into them. Put them down, not honour them
Give them a piece of my mind.
I would want to deal with it – harshly.


Jesus is cut from a different cloth. A cloth he invites us to put on too.

*Whoever wants to be great among you, must be your servant.*[133]

Right at the start of this passage, it tells us that Jesus is completely comfortable in his own identity. He lives in the freedom that comes from knowing that God has put *everything* under his power. He knows where he comes from and he knows where he's going.
What will Jesus do with this knowledge?
This freedom?

And then comes the connective. The word that links this sentence to the next. And that word is 'so'.
Therefore.
Because of this.
Jesus has *all* this power. He has *all* this freedom. He knows his past and his future. So…
He gets up, wraps a towel around his waist, pours a basin of water and begins washing their feet!
This is the height of humility.
The epitome of servanthood.
The foundation of incredible resilience.

*****

What Jesus is doing here, is demonstrating a way of living that seems completely paradoxical to our modern way of thinking. We live in a society that says that we need to work our way upwards into positions of leadership so that we can be the boss, others can serve us and the more people we can tell what to do, the more satisfaction and significance we will experience.
Jesus' alternative approach tells us that true freedom, true life satisfaction will come when we let go of this way of thinking and approach people and situations with the attitude of a servant.

Paul, taking on this alternative kingdom approach, writes to the church in Philippi with the following advice:

*Do nothing out of selfish ambition or vain conceit. Rather, in humility value others above yourselves, not looking to your own interests but each of you to the interests of the others.*[134]

Jesus is using this opportunity of washing his disciple's feet to foreshadow the greatest act of servanthood, humility and sacrifice ever committed. At the cross, Jesus demonstrates perfect love, and we see the relationship between sacrifice and love most perfectly in Jesus' death. He is our model.

Paul, describing Jesus' nature, puts it this way:

*Who, being in very nature God,*
*did not consider equality with God something to be used to his own advantage;*
*rather, he made himself nothing*
*by taking the very nature of a servant,*
*being made in human likeness.*
*And being found in appearance as a man,*
*he humbled himself*
*by becoming obedient to death —*
*even death on a cross!*[135]

Talk about humility.
Jesus was equal with God! Yet he lowered himself completely and utterly. This had absolutely nothing to do with humanity being deserving.
It wasn't because we are good.
In fact, it wasn't about us at all.
It was about *His* nature.
*His* love.
*His* sacrifice.

Which paid for our freedom.

This is the example that Jesus is setting his disciples (and by extension, it's the example he is setting us). We know it's easier to love the people who love us. That's not the level of love we are called to.
Whose feet did Jesus wash?
Peter's, John's, James' and all the disciples.
Including the feet of Judas.

Jesus stood in front of the man who, in just a few moments, is about to exit the room in order to betray him, to death, for money.
He knelt down, looked into Judas' eyes, held his betrayer's feet gently in his hands and lovingly washed away the grime.
How could he do this?
Because it wasn't about Judas at all.
It was about Jesus.
And the people he is inviting us to be.

*****

Paul, in that letter to the Philippian church we just read, describes Jesus' humility, but the sentence preceding that states:

*In your relationships with one another, have the same mindset as Christ Jesus:*[136]

If we just 'oooh' and 'aaah' about the amazing love, humility, sacrifice and servanthood of Jesus then we're missing the point completely. The point is that Jesus gives an example for
us to follow.
In *all* your dealings with *all* people, *be like Jesus.*

And the truth is, we wouldn't be instructed to love this way if we didn't have the capacity to love this way. The presence of the Holy Spirit in us gives us the ability to live and love like Jesus did. In fact, Jesus himself said, *'whoever believes in me will do the works I have been doing, and they will do even greater things than these, because I am going to the Father.*[137]

Can you imagine what this world would look like if this was our approach to every relationship we had?
Can you imagine what our marriages would be like if we approached them in this way – humbly and sacrificially? Wanting the absolute best for our husband or wife? Lowering ourselves completely for them? Not because they are deserving, because the truth is, they're not. But because of who you are. Because of the capacity for love that has been put inside of you.

Can you imagine what our families would look like if we approached loving in this way?
Can you imagine what our friendships, or our workplaces would look like?

*****

The story is told of a beggar who asks for alms from Alexander the Great as he and his entourage pass by. The beggar is poor and wretched and has no right or claim upon the ruler, yet the king throws him several gold coins. A courtier, astonished at his generosity, looks up at Alexander and comments, "Sir, copper coins would surely meet a beggar's need."
Alexander responds with true dignity, "Truly, copper coins would suit the beggar's need, but gold coins suit Alexander's giving."

We love, not according to the needs, or the character, or suitability, or the deserving nature of others. We love according to the example we have been given and according to the capacity that has been placed within us.

And as we do, that capacity will grow and grow.

*****

So, Jesus, having explained to his disciples in words about achieving greatness through serving, now tells them again...with his actions. He's told them the truth, now he shows them the truth. He rises up, takes off his outer robe, puts a towel around himself, fetches a pot of water and begins to wash their dirty feet. I wonder how his disciples felt in this moment.

Awestruck.

Speechless.

Devastated and ashamed of themselves!

Their Rabbi and master, the one Peter has acknowledged as the Christ, is on his knees and performing an act that only the lowest slave would do.

Jesus' cousin, John (the Baptist) actually said,

*'I baptize with water...but among you stands one you do not know. He is the one who comes after me, the straps of whose sandals I am not worthy to untie.'*[138]

Peter (as always) is the one who finally has to say something. He can't hold it in any longer,

*"Lord are you going to wash my feet?...No...you shall never wash my feet!"*[139]

The language that headstrong Peter uses is the strongest possible.

No.

Never in all eternity.

No way under no circumstances will you ever do this thing.

Take it to the bank.

It ain't gonna happen!

*"Unless I wash you, you have no part with me."*

*"Then, Lord," Simon Peter replied, "not just my feet but my hands and my head as well!"*[140]

Don't you think that Peter is awesome! He lives his whole life *all in*. He starts with 'Never!' and then in a heartbeat changes to, 'Oh okay then. But don't just wash my feet, wash everything.'
He is so desperate to get it right and He is only saying what the others are thinking. He was only saying what you or I would be thinking. And so, he performs his liguistic U-turn on a sixpence.

If this is how it has to be, then Lord, wash it all! I can imagine him starting to strip off his clothes even as he is speaking the words!

*****

What did Jesus mean when he said, 'Unless I wash you, you have no part with me'?

The whole of this foot washing account is an illustration. Not only is it in example of how we should treat others, it is a foreshadow of what Jesus was about to do. It's a representation of His humility, sacrifice and loving action. He is explaining to Peter, 'You don't understand it. You don't get it right now, but you will later on. After the next few days have taken place and you've had time to consider this, you will realize that what I'm doing has eternal significance.

Peter, you think I'm making myself low by doing this, but I'm about to go down ever lower. I'm about to go lower than anybody ever has. As low as it's possible to go. Because of my love.
Peter... you can't stop this humiliation.'

Jesus is saying that unless he washes you, you have no part with him. If you want a relationship with God, it has to be through Jesus. He is the *only way* that you can be cleansed. There is no salvation or forgiveness or eternity apart from Jesus.

So of course, Peter replies, 'Yes! That's what I want. Give me the full scrub!'

*'Those who have had a bath need only to wash their feet; their whole body is clean. And you are clean'*[41]

Peter you are clean! He's essentially saying to him, Peter - you are already saved. When you've been cleansed, you don't need to be cleansed again. When you are saved, you don't need to be saved again. But, as you go on your journey, your feet pick up dirt and dust and you need to have your feet washed.

So, what does this mean for us - well once we have given our lives to Jesus. We are fully washed, we are cleansed – not because of our own righteous living but because of the righteousness that is given to us, through Jesus' death.

When Jesus says we are righteous. It's not referring to our performance, it's referring to our position. It is not because we are deserving, but because Jesus is full of grace and mercy. We are clean – we don't need to be cleansed again.

However, on the journey of life we slip up.

We take wrong turns.

We sin. (Well I do at least).

So, we continually confess our sins and Jesus goes on cleansing us from all unrighteousness. He stoops down and washes the grime from our feet.

Every time we come.

*****

So, we see Jesus, confident in his identity and power, demonstrating ultimate resilience by loving humbly and sacrificially.
As a servant.

*Now that you know these things, you will be blessed if you do them.*[142]

Two important statements here:
1. You know these things.

This is definite. A statement of fact. You know these things because I have both taught you and shown you.

2. You will be blessed if you do them.

This is less certain. You need to take action based on what you know, in order to get the desired result (a blessed life).

I wonder if many of us live our life in this gap. The gap between *knowing* what we should do and actually doing it.

We know how we're supposed to live.
We know how we're supposed to love.
We know that we should approach our relationships with the attitude of a servant.
However, it's hard to put this into practice. We fall into the world's way of operating, joining the rat-race to the top of the pile instead of racing to the back of the line. Arguing over who is the greatest, rather than washing each other's feet.

Jesus promises that if we can actually live this way, there is a blessing.
Do you want God's blessing on your life?
Of course you do!
So, try another way.

Be confident in your own God-given identity and then live humbly, sacrificially and selflessly. Like a foot-washing servant.

This could be the beginning of true resilience in your life.

# Chapter 11
# Leave Your Boat

*For the Spirit God gave us does not make us timid,*
*but gives us power, love and self-discipline.*
*2 Timothy 1:7*

Two facts about me that you might not know:

Fact 1. I love watching movies.
Fact 2. I'm a bit of an introvert.

So - one of my absolute favourite things to do on a day off, is to head to the local cinema, by myself, to catch the latest releases.

I have a bit of a routine on these rare and special excursions! I make myself a latte in a travel mug, put together one or two snacks in a bag (you might call me a cheapskate – I like to think of myself as sensible for not paying inflated cinema prices!). I skip happily to the cinema with my coffee and snacks, and I spend a couple of blissful hours in my own company, losing myself in a good film.
That is heaven right there.

Now I like all kinds of movies; thrillers, action movies, suspense filled dramas, comedy, even romcoms (if there is nothing else on). But I particularly enjoy disaster movies.
Epic films where *BIG* stuff happens. Whole cities get obliterated, skyscrapers are reduced to rubble. Whole countries or even entire planets are in mortal danger of getting wiped out.
Until the hero (or superhero) arrives to save the day.

135

What I've noticed is that these films will pretty much always finish with some kind of happy ending. Even after all the destruction. Half the planet has been wiped out or maimed. Cities are lying in rubble. However, the filmmaker always wants to leave the viewer with hope. With something almost inanely positive.

There's a great film I watched at the cinema a few years ago with Dwayne (The Rock) Johnson[143]. This was a disaster movie on steroids! The whole West Coast of the United States gets pretty much destroyed by a freak earthquake, bringing death and mayhem to millions of people. Then, right at the end of the film there is a scene with Dwayne Johnson's character and his family. His bruised and battered son turns to him and asks the obvious question, 'What are we going to do now, Dad?'

Then Dwayne, looking out into the distant, pauses for a moment as the music swells and the camera pans across the carnage and destruction replies with typical heroic intensity, 'We're going to rebuild!'

It's really cheesy!
This is the end that played well with test audiences?
Of course it is, I lapped it up!
We (the viewers) don't want to be left without hope.

I want you to imagine, for a moment, that the ending of the film had taken a different tack...
'What are we going to do now, Dad?'
Dwayne Johnson, crying like a baby, screams hysterically 'I've got no idea— we're all going to die!'
FADE TO BLACK.

That just wouldn't work. We want a healthy dollop of hope and optimism in our movies.

*****

What I have realised is that when you have a happy, optimistic ending, you soon forget all the pain and destruction you just witnessed.
The ending is crucial to how a story is remembered.

Another great line from another great but very different movie, announces:

*"Everything will be alright in the end so if it is not alright, it is not yet the end."*[144]

It is the job of resilience to get you safely to the end of your story. Whatever you are going through. Whatever troubles and heartaches you feel you are stranded in right now, it's your resilience that is going to get you through it - and get through it well.

In the previous chapters we have learned a number of key principles, mostly taken from scripture, which you can apply directly to your own life in order to strengthen resilience. Principles such as forgiveness, hope, praise, gratitude, generosity, community and service, when built into the fabric of your life, will put you in a more advantageous position when the proverbial poop hits the proverbial fan.

Which it will.
And you know it.

So, well done for making it this far, and I want to encourage you to keep going. There are a few more principles I want to share that I think will help you, because they have helped me in my own story.

*****

Many of the characters we meet in the bible had mishaps and missteps along their journey. Almost every single one took wrong turns on their way to becoming the man or woman of faith that we remember from our Sunday school classes.

The apostle, Peter, is no exception.

With hindsight, we can judge many of Peter's actions in the light of the man he became in the second half of his life. Which was very different to the first half.

There is a remarkable transition from a gruff, outspoken, hot-tempered, fisherman who constantly battles with 'foot in mouth' disease. Inappropriate statements and tactless action are bread and butter to this favourite of Jesus. And yet later in his life we find a bold, humble, diplomatic and obedient servant of Jesus. Obedient even to his own death.

History tells us that Peter chose to be crucified upside down because he felt unworthy to be crucified the same as his Lord, Jesus.

This lowly, uneducated fisherman becomes a 'fisher of men' whose gospel message shaped and changed our world forever.

We can glimpse Peter's journey throughout the four gospels and feel deeply encouraged about the setbacks in our own journey. In Peter's story we find a number of events - defining moments - that transformed him into the 'rock' (his name literally means 'rock'... I wonder if Dwayne Johnson's middle name is Peter?!) he was to become, shaping his faith, his maturity and his resilience. These events become simply a stepping-stone to fulfilling God's purposes and plans.

In one particular event, Peter and the other disciples have just witnessed Jesus' miracle – the feeding of thousands of people (five thousand men, besides women and children[145]) with two fish and five loaves of bread. Jesus intends to cross over the Sea of Galilee, and he makes the disciples get in a boat and go ahead of him, while he ascends a mountain alone to pray.

A storm arises on the lake. The water's getting pretty choppy and the boat is being buffeted by the waves because the wind is against it. This is how the disciples spend the night while Jesus is up on the mountainside praying. Maybe you remember what happens next:

*Shortly before dawn Jesus went out to them, walking on the lake. When the disciples saw him walking on the lake, they were terrified. "It's a ghost," they said, and cried out in fear.*
*But Jesus immediately said to them: "Take courage! It is I. Don't be afraid."*
*"Lord, if it's you," Peter replied, "tell me to come to you on the water."*
*"Come," he said.*
*Then Peter got down out of the boat, walked on the water and came toward Jesus. But when he saw the wind, he was afraid and, beginning to sink, cried out, "Lord, save me!"*
*Immediately Jesus reached out his hand and caught him. "You of little faith," he said, "why did you doubt?"*
*And when they climbed into the boat, the wind died down. Then those who were in the boat worshiped him, saying, "Truly you are the Son of God."*[146]

Why is this such a defining moment for Peter? There are a number of important truths that Peter learned through his experience that night which I imagine bolstered and sustained him in the roller-coaster years ahead of him.

And there's a few things we can learn from this event too. I don't imagine that walking on water is a skill that you are going to need to master in your lifetime. However, I am confident that *that* feeling of dread and uncertainty is something you will have to face at some point in your future.
So, Peter, what can you teach us?!

This incident is also described in Mark's and John's gospels. From these other perspectives of the same event, we can glean some extra, useful pieces of information.

139

John, describing this episode, explains that the crowd, following Jesus' miracle with the two fish and five loaves, wants to make him their king. I guess this is why Jesus immediately sends his disciples off, dismisses the crowd and goes up a mountain by himself to pray. In order to keep his heart right and to maintain his perspective, he needs time with his father. As we've looked at in previous chapters, resilience is forged in humility and keeping a proper perspective of yourself, and your position in God's eyes, is crucial to navigating your way through the troubles of life.

So, Jesus sends away the potential distractions and gets on his knees before his father.

The Disciples, meanwhile, have been obedient to Jesus' instructions. They have pushed out onto the lake in their boat and immediately found themselves in the centre of a storm. How many of us know that obedience is not a guarantee that we will be spared adversity? Trouble exists as a natural part of living, indeed some troubles that we face are there to teach us, grow us and shape us into a better, more resilient version of ourselves.

In Mark's account we read:

*Later that night, the boat was in the middle of the lake, and he was alone on land. He saw the disciples straining at the oars, because the wind was against them.*[147]

And then:

*Shortly before dawn he went out to them, walking on the lake.*[148]

There's this period of time - a critical gap - between: **'Later that night'** and **'Shortly before dawn'**.

This is the space where the disciples feel like they are facing their troubles alone. I expect they are thinking, "Where is Jesus right now? He told us to do this and now we have to face hurricane winds and thirty foot waves without him?"

This is a gap that everybody finds themselves in at difficult points in their life. Maybe you are in that gap right now. Perhaps you will find yourself in it next week or next year. If you are living the grand adventure of faith, there will almost certainly be a time when you are obediently straining against the wind, waiting for Jesus to show up.
Riding a storm that is challenging your every sinew.
Facing wind and waves that you are straining against.
Trying to overcome circumstances that are threatening to capsize your life.

Your head tells you that Jesus must be with you, because you were obedient to his call and he brought you to this place, and yet circumstances feel like they could overwhelm you at any moment.

Perhaps the words of the worship song 'Still' are going through your mind:

*When the oceans rise and thunders roar.*
*I will soar with You above the storm.*
*Father you are King over the flood.*
*I will be still and know You are God.*[149]

The sentiment is wonderful. Of course, God *can* lift us above the storms of life, but our experience tells us that it doesn't always happen like this straight way. Often, we go *through* the storms and come out the other side stronger and more resilient.

Maybe the song 'Cornerstone' is more appropriate to your current situation:

141

*When darkness seems to hide His face.*
*I rest on his unchanging Grace*
*In every high and stormy gale*
*My anchor holds within the veil…*
*…Through the storm, He is Lord, Lord of all.*[150]

Where's Jesus whilst we are in the middle of the storm? We can be confident that he's watching over us. He hasn't left us alone. His presence is assured and he will step in at exactly the right moment. In the meantime, he is joyful at seeing us grow, get stretched, develop and mature, becoming authentic disciples as we develop more and more resilience. Remember the 'Rocky' montage we talked about in chapter three? Perhaps the only way to get through the next big fight that's around the corner is by getting through the tough 'training' challenges we are in right now. So get chopping wood!

*****

Jesus' brother James demonstrates that he understands this all too well when he writes:

*Consider it pure joy, my brothers and sisters, whenever you face trials of many kinds, because you know that the testing of your faith produces perseverance. Let perseverance finish its work so that you may be mature and complete, not lacking anything.*[151]

We face tests and trials of many kinds, not to see if we pass or fail, but to build and *prove* our resilience. The Greek word translated *testing* - 'dokimion' – can also be translated *proving* or *proven genuine*.
When we come through the storm, we can see that our faith is proved genuine, which equips us for whatever test or trial may be coming up next.

That's why we consider it *pure joy*! The storms are often God's ways of bringing us to maturity.

I remember when our second son (JJ) was born with a congenital heart condition and spent a large portion of his early years in hospital undergoing a number of difficult open-heart surgeries. For us, as his parents, it was certainly difficult. You might even call it *trials of many kinds*. However, we both felt such a deep and unshakable peace, despite the circumstances, as we learned to trust God's hand on our family's life.

As we look back at this difficult period in our lives, we realise that in the most challenging moments, we discovered something which we wouldn't have discovered had we not had to go through it:

Our faith in God works!

Am I saying that God caused JJ's heart problems so that I would have a stronger, more resilient faith? No, of course I wouldn't say that. However, I do believe God can use all circumstances (good or ill) for ultimate good, and the proving of my faith during these troubles has made me more resilient, faith-filled and assured of my hope in God.

*****

There are potentially twelve disciples in the boat. They've all had a rough night. They've been rowing for their lives and are tired and worn out. Then, amidst the screaming wind, the rolling waves and the spray stinging their faces, someone spots a figure walking across the water in their direction.
Panic ensues.
They think it's a ghost.
They cry out in fear! Of course, they do. Their nerves are already shredded. As my teenage kids would say, "They're bare stressed out!"

So Jesus calls out to them to not be afraid. To have courage.

These two concepts go hand in hand.
Have courage.
Don't be afraid.
These are two of the most common commands in the bible.[152]

Twelve in the boat.
Jesus has just revealed himself and is walking towards them.
Most of them are baffled, afraid and dumbstruck.
One of them is about to respond. Of course, it's Peter.

*"Lord if it's you…command me to come to you on the water"*[153]

This is a really important verse.
This account is not simply about taking risks. Any fool can do that and end up in heap of trouble. I know because I have been that fool many times!

It's a lesson about obedience.
It's about authentic discipleship.
It's about having courage, undergirded by the knowledge that you are walking in step with the will of God.
Yes, we do need courage to take risks.
We need to not fear the storms.
But we also need the wisdom and discernment to hear, understand and follow God's call.

Put yourself in Peter's 'size 10s' for just a moment. Picture the storm raging around you, the towering waves, the howling of the wind, the pitching of the boat, the creaking of the timbers, the tiredness seeping into your bones. Despite all these feelings and very real dangers, inside the boat is still considerably safer than outside the boat. There is still a measure of comfort and security by staying exactly where you are. I suppose that's why the other disciples didn't respond in the same way as Peter.

What would you choose? The dangerous water? Or the secure boat?
If you get out of the boat, there is every possibility you are going to sink.
But if you don't get out of the boat, there is an absolute guaranteed certainty that you will not walk on the water.

Right now, we should all ask ourselves this question:
What is my boat?
What's the thing that represents my safety and security apart from God himself.

My boat is whatever I am tempted to put my trust in, especially when life gets stormy.
So, what's the comfort in your life?
What is it that keeps you from joining Jesus on the waves?
What is it that most produces fear in you – especially when you think of leaving it behind and stepping out in faith?

*The decision to grow always involves a choice between risk and comfort. This means that to be a follower of Jesus you must renounce comfort as the ultimate value of your life.*[154]

Your boat could be your vocation or career, a relationship, an addiction, trying to please your parents, success and riches; there is a long list of 'boats' that could be preventing you living God's best life.

There's a moment in the Gospels where a rich young ruler is invited by Jesus to step out of his boat:

*"Go, sell everything you have and give to the poor, and you will have treasure in heaven. Then come, follow me."*[155]

In a way, the rich young man's question was similar to Peter's, "If it is you Lord, tell me to come."

Jesus invites the rich young man to come, but his 'boat' is too comfortable. The voice of comfort and danger speaks louder to him than Jesus' invitation and tragically, he declines the opportunity.

Jesus tells Peter to come.
So Peter does.

I think in this moment, Peter is able to switch off his rational brain for a few seconds, reach deep down to find the courage he needs and allow childlike faith to guide his actions.
He walks towards Jesus.
On the water.

And then he doesn't.

He becomes distracted by the elements around him and sinks into the water, crying out,

*"Lord save me!"*[156]

In this moment, he doesn't have time for a lengthy plea, or a, "If it's you Lord…"
Now it's simply, "HELP!"

Did Peter fail?
That's really the question isn't it?
And I think the honest answer is:
Yes.

And no.

Certainly, Jesus rebuked him for his lack of faith

*"You of little faith, why did you doubt?"*[57]

Peter moved his eyes off where they should have been, and he sank into the water. In this way, he failed. His doubts were too strong. In this moment, his circumstances loomed larger than his faith. The storm was still raging around him. It's important that we notice that Jesus didn't calm the storm before he told Peter to come.
Maybe we are sometimes sitting in the boat and waiting for the storm to subside before we step out, rather than trusting Jesus' call to us.

All the other disciples stayed safely in the boat. They weren't doing anything wrong as such. It's not like they committed a grave sin by not stepping out.
But in a way they were far bigger failures than Peter was.
They failed privately and it's far easier to fail privately than publicly.

Only Peter out of the twelve knew the shame of public failure. Messing up in front of the crowd.
Only Peter out of the twelve knew two other things also:

1.  The miracle and excitement of actually walking on the surface of water. He would never forget that feeling.
Ever.

The feel of the water under his feet. The movement of the waves. The thrill of breaking the laws of physics.

2.  Peter also experienced personally the hand of Jesus lifting him up and saving him in a moment of desperate need.

I find it interesting that the next verse says:

*And when they climbed into the boat…* [158]

What occurred between Jesus taking the sinking Peter by the hand and then climbing into the boat?

Do you think he dragged Peter, spluttering and half submerged, through the water to the boat? Or did Jesus lift him up, hold his hand and then walk next to him across the rolling sea to the side, before they climbed into the boat together.

In my imagination, it's the second scenario that makes most sense. Jesus and Peter walking together back to the gawking, shivering disciples.

As Peter navigated the challenges of the second half of his life, these were two experiences that nobody could ever take from him.

Resilience is built in the storms of life. Don't allow your earthly comforts and security prevent you from becoming the version of yourself that God is calling you to.

Be ready to leave the comfort of what you know and step into a life of challenge and adventure, where storms will be present, but so will God's strength. Your courage and your resilience and your faith will grow and grow as you become an authentic disciple of Jesus.

Fix your eyes on Jesus.
Get ready to step out of your boat.

# Chapter 12
# It's All About Me

*'Anyone who wants to live all out for Christ is in for a lot of trouble; there's no getting around it...But don't let it faze you. Stick with what you learned and believed, sure of the integrity of your teachers'*
2 Timothy 3:12,14 (The Message Bible)

Looking at the world around us (currently in lockdown because of the Covid 19 pandemic), it's easy to become overwhelmed by the troubles we see. We are viewing everything through the narrow lens of the TV and the internet. We are, in effect, hostage to the news that we see on our screens. A news cycle that is decided by people who have their own agenda and can instil fear in us if we don't engage with it in a measured, resilient, God-centred way.

Conspiracy theories abound with regards to what has caused the pandemic - who's at fault - where the blame should fall.
There are numerous opinions about what needs to happen to make the world right again.
Political division and one-upmanship. As soon as one politician or scientist says, 'this is the problem', there are a hundred voices disagreeing and offering alternative and even contradictory opinions.

Every country seems to have a different approach, dealing with the pandemic in diverse ways. And again, politicians and leaders use this as an opportunity to have a go, find fault, to pull 'the other side' down.

It's hard for us to separate truth from lies, fact from fiction and it can leave us dangling in the wind if we lack the resilience to tether our thoughts to something solid and unchanging.

So, what do we do?

Do we try and wade through the mire of information? Attempt to get an accurate picture of what's really going on? Do we believe everyone? Do we believe no one? Do we find an excuse to batten down the hatches and not engage at all with global issues?

Whilst it's useful (and probably the right thing) to interact with the issues affecting the world around us, it's important not to get bogged down with conspiracy theories, gossip and the endless cycle of finger-pointing and blame-mongering. The answer to all these things is to keep the *finger of change* pointed directly at yourself.

It's all about me!

That's really the only thing I ultimately have any control over.
No matter what is going on around me...
No matter what anybody else is doing or saying...
No matter how big the trouble or dark the tunnel I find myself in... there are right decisions and wrong decisions and I should simply ask myself the question, 'What's the right thing for *me* to do in this situation?'.

In the movie *Frozen II*, it's a question that the protagonist, Anna, asks herself when she finds herself in difficulties that are bigger than she can handle:

*I've seen dark before, but not like this*
*This is cold, this is empty, this is numb*
*The life I knew is over, the lights are out*
*Hello, darkness, I'm ready to succumb*
*I follow you around, I always have*
*But you've gone to a place I cannot find*
*This grief has a gravity, it pulls me down*

*But a tiny voice whispers in my mind*
*You are lost, hope is gone*
*But you must go on*
*And do the next right thing*[159]

I've found that popular movies often have universal themes simmering beneath the storyline that reaches into the depths of what it means to be human. This one is no exception. The only thing I would add to this idea is to *Yield to God's ways* and do the next right thing.
That's all we really need to do.

It sounds simple, doesn't it? And it kind of *is* simple in concept, just not so much in execution.
But the truth is, if everybody just did this…well I don't know what would happen, but I bet the world would look completely different to how it does right now.

*****

King David, writing in the Psalms said it like this:

*As for me, I will always have hope, I will praise you more and more*[160]

As for me…

This is a turning point for David in this psalm. Like many of us, he is observing the world around him and he is troubled by it. Bible commentators speculate that this particular Psalm was written when David's own son, Absalom, was rebelling against him and trying to steal his throne.

In the preceding verses, David is saying things like:
my enemies speak against me…those who wait to kill me conspire together… David mentions his accusers and those who want to harm

him… He expresses his emotions about feeling far from God… He is losing his strength… And then he says:

*'As for me'.*

It's like he is shutting out the rest of the world for this brief moment and focusing only on himself. His own actions.

All this is going on around me.
It's hard and I can't solve it.
It's too big for me to get my head around, but…
'As for me, I will always have hope'
This is a great approach for us too. To think and act in this way needs wisdom. It needs a transformed mind and it needs resilience.

The issues around us can seem overwhelming, particularly if you are someone who is disposed to problem solving. Maybe, for a moment – just shut out the big issues of this world and say, 'As for me, this is the next right thing that I'm going to do. I can't fix Covid 19. I can't end the global lockdown. I can't control unemployment or the shrinking economy and I don't have the answers to the international issues that face the global population. But…
As for me, this is what I can do.
This is what I can control.
I can do the next right thing.

For King David in this moment, the next right thing was to remain hopeful and to praise more and more. And this thought takes David's thinking down a whole new path.

*'My mouth will tell of your righteous deeds,*
*of your saving acts all day long'*
*'I will come and proclaim your mighty acts, Sovereign Lord;'*
*'Since my youth, God, you have taught me,'*
*'Your righteousness, God, reaches to the heavens,*

*you who have done great things.'*
*'Who is like you, God?'*
*'you will restore my life again;*
*You will increase my honour*
*and comfort me once more.'*[161]

The three words, 'As for me', serve as a pivot point in David's thinking. It's the moment where, after looking at all the troubles that surround him, he shifts his focus to a positive place. It helps him to change his story.

\*\*\*\*\*

When I was growing up there was a series of books called 'Choose your own adventure' books. The stories were mostly fantasy fiction about young people wondering through magical worlds, meeting mysterious characters, both good and bad, and there was usually some kind of mystery that needed solving. What made these books different was that at the end of each chapter there would typically be a cliff-hanger, a defining moment in the narrative and a choice of two options. Each of these options would take the reader to a different page and continue the narrative from there.

So, for example, you would reach a point in the story where you found yourself facing a cave troll, armed with a deadly looking, sharp, three-pronged pitchfork, and you would have to decide whether you were going to either; a) face the foul beast and attempt to overpower it (turn to page 39), or b) turn around and run back the way you came screaming like a ninny (turn to page 43).

Each of the two options would result in different consequences and then further choices in the subsequent pages. In this way, the reader could 'choose their own adventure.' It sounds a lot more exciting than it actually was. I was always somewhat disappointed because the story would invariably finish very quickly (i.e. you would die, impaled on a pitchfork, or succeed in your quest in just a few pages!)

What I *did* like about the books was the sense of control I had over the characters and the storyline. My own destiny was in my power.

Our lives are a little bit like those *Choose Your Own Adventure* books. Every moment provides us with options to respond to the world around us and each decision leads to a further crossroads of choices. In all honesty we don't really know which ones are the life-changing decisions. All we can do is choose wisely in each moment and face the consequence of that choice (pitchfork-wielding cave troll or treasure-finding success!).

We do the next right thing.
We look at the choices before us and we say, "As for me..."

These three significant words occur many times throughout the bible. Let's highlight a few and apply some useful life-lessons in the process that will help us make better choices and grow in wisdom and resilience.

*****

## Joshua

Towards the end of his long and eventful life, Joshua gathers the elders, leaders, judges and officials of Israel and reminds them of the miraculous journey they've been on: Surviving the plagues, escape from slavery in Egypt, crossing *through* the red sea, wondering in the wilderness, crossing the Jordan river and taking the city of Jericho and many other amazing achievements. He lists all the victories that God has given the nation of Israel and he reminds them of the wonderful

Promised Land that they have now inhabited. He ends with this great statement:

*But if serving the LORD seems undesirable to you, then choose for yourselves this day whom you will serve, whether the gods your ancestors served beyond the Euphrates, or the gods of the Amorites, in whose land you are living. But as for me and my household, we will serve the LORD."*[162]

[Joshua drops the mic and exits, stage left!]

I love the clarity of this statement. Joshua is not losing sleep about the choices that are out of his control. He is totally focused on his own decisions.

This is where we've come from.
This is how God has shown his faithfulness to us time and time again.
But it's your choice what you do with that. You can focus on what's going on around you. You can conform to the pattern of this world if you want to. You can choose this god or that god.
You can spend your time in pursuits that don't ultimately have value.
You can half kill yourself trying to control or manipulate others to choose well.
You can waste your time and energy striving for things that the world around you tells you is important.

Or you can choose *your own* adventure. You can decide for yourself to do the next right thing.
But *as for me* and my family, we will serve the Lord.

I can't control the decisions and choices you make. But as for me…this is what I'm going to do. Choosing to serve God wholeheartedly is the next right choice for me to make.

\*\*\*\*\*

## Abraham's servant

The patriarch, Abraham, sends his servant on a mission to find a wife for his son, Isaac. The servant proceeds on a long and arduous journey and he pleads with God,

*"Make me successful… show kindness to my master Abraham."*[163]

Before he has even finished praying, a young and beautiful girl, Rebekah comes out to the well and offers him and his camels some water.

*Then the man bowed down and worshiped the LORD, saying, "Praise be to the LORD, the God of my master Abraham, who has not abandoned his kindness and faithfulness to my master.*
*As for me, the LORD has led me on the journey to the house of my master's relatives."*[164]

Boom! God scores again!
As for me, the Lord has led me…

What do I have to do for the Lord to lead me?
I have to be ready and willing to follow.
This is a great prayer for all of us: 'Lord lead me. Guide my steps. Show me the right path. Give me the right thoughts.'

*Your word is a lamp to my feet and a light to my path*[165]

Therefore, I'm going to read the word and expect revelation and insight for the steps I should take.

I'm going to listen, respond and obey the prompting of the Holy Spirit in my life.

*As for me*, I will follow wherever the Lord leads and trust that his presence will go with me.

*****

## Samuel

Yet another fellow coming towards the end of his life, Samuel the prophet, gives a farewell speech to the leaders and influencers in the nation of Israel:

*"I have listened to everything you said to me and have set a king over you. Now you have a king as your leader. As for me, I am old and grey, and my sons are here with you. I have been your leader from my youth until this day.*[166]

He then, just like Joshua before him, recounts all of the amazing things that God has done. He chastises them for many of the decisions they have made. Fear grips the people because of the sins they have committed towards God and they ask Samuel to pray for them. Samuel responds:

*"As for me, far be it from me that I should sin against the LORD by failing to pray for you. And I will teach you the way that is good and right."*[167]

[Samuel acknowledges the crowd's wild applause and walks off slowly, into the sunset]

As for me, even though I'm getting old and I'm no longer as able as I was - I can no longer travel the length and breadth of Israel helping you like I have done all my life - but what I can do is to not stop praying for you.

Your choices and your decisions are out of my control but *as for me*, I won't stop praying. In fact, he says he won't sin against the Lord by not praying.

This is definitely something we all can and should say...'I don't have the ability to fix the nation's issues or even my regional or local issues. I don't even have the ability to fix some of the issues in my own home. But, as for me, I can keep on praying. I can keep bringing the people around me and the issues to God – because I know he CAN help and He DOES have answers.

The wonderful thing about praying for others is that it not only has the potential of altering their situations, it also invariably transforms me. It brings me closer to God and to the people I'm praying for. A purposeful and consistent prayer life is one of the most effective tools in building my resilience.

*****

**Asaph**

It's another Psalm but this time it's not David, it's a temple worker called Asaph, a guy who wrote twelve out of the one hundred and fifty Psalms we have in our bibles.

This Psalm is so helpful for us. It's slightly different to all the other 'as for me' examples we've looked at. In the previous examples (David's, Joshua's, Abraham's and Samuel's) they begin by looking at the trouble in the outside world - the big issues that are bearing down on them from outside, and then the phrase 'as for me' is used to pivot the attention from outside, toward themselves.

In this Psalm, Asaph is describing his *internal* struggles, the crisis he is going through in his own mind. He uses phrases like,

*"My feet had almost slipped...I envied the prosperity of those around me... Surely in vain I kept my heart pure...All day long I have been afflicted...When my heart was grieved and my spirit embittered, I was senseless and ignorant."*[168]

Asaph pours out all these internal struggles he is battling with. He is losing the battle with his own mind and all these thoughts are tying him up in knots.

How often have we done exactly the same thing? We get pulled down into a pit of negative thinking, spiralling down, feeling sorry for ourselves, organising a 'pity party' and we don't know how to pull ourselves out.

It's not just the pressures from outside of us that can trip us up. It's not just the global issues that heap trouble into our laps. It's the place we allow our mind to go to, that prevents us living the free life that God has for us. When Jesus said, "In this world, you will have trouble", I'm pretty sure he included the trouble we bring on ourselves by not having a healthy pattern of thinking.

Then Asaph finds his breakthrough...

*Yet I am always with you;*
*you hold me by my right hand.*
*You guide me with your counsel,*
*and afterward you will take me into glory.*
*Whom have I in heaven but you?*
*And earth has nothing I desire besides you.*
*My flesh and my heart may fail,*
*but God is the strength of my heart*
*and my portion forever.*
*Those who are far from you will perish;*
*you destroy all who are unfaithful to you.*

*But **as for me**, it is good to be near God.*[169]

Yes Asaph! – You got there, buddy!

As for me, I'm going to place myself near God. I'm going to put myself in His proximity. I'm going to make sure my relationship with him is of primary importance.
As for me, I have discovered the goodness and the blessing that comes from drawing near to God.
What happens when we draw near to God? He draws near to us!

Even when I am facing all these internal battles. Even when I can't see the light at the end of the tunnel. Even when it feels like I don't have answers to the big questions that life throws at me. As for me – I'm going to stay close to God.

Britain's Prime Minister during the Second World War, Winston Churchill, wrote a lot of speeches and quotable sayings. He had a way with words that really travelled to the heart of the issue. One of his often-quoted remarks is this:

*Out of intense complexities, intense simplicities emerge.*[170]

This 'as for me…' approach to decisions, is a prime example of this idea. It's intensely simple. It removes the pressure of taking responsibility for things that are ultimately outside your control and provides a simple solution to the complex troubles that you might be facing – either from outside or from within.

What's the next right decision?
What's the next right step?
What is God, through the Holy Spirit directing you to do?
What is everyone else doing, or advising you to do, that you should ignore?

160

Everyone else can choose a different path but as for me...

...I will always have hope.
...I will serve the Lord.
...I will follow His lead.
...I will keep praying for people and circumstances.
...I will stay near to His presence.

The art of resilience is keeping your thinking straightforward, and your actions simple.

Just do the next right thing.

## Epilogue
# What's the Point of Resilience?

*Though the fig tree does not bud*
*and there are no grapes on the vines,*
*though the olive crop fails*
*and the fields produce no food,*
*though there are no sheep in the pen*
*and no cattle in the stalls,*
*yet I will rejoice in the Lord,*
*I will be joyful in God my Saviour.*
*Habakkuk 3:17-18*

As I sit down to begin writing this final chapter, the need for resilience is hitting home in a particularly stark and tangible way. Yesterday, in a hospital waiting room, facemask on, sitting a 'Covid-secure', two metre distance from the other patients, waiting to get the results of a skin cancer test, my thoughts were on the contents of this book.

I have spent the past few months writing about 'thriving' in adversity, 'taking heart' when trouble hits, 'finding hope' in the storms of life. Are these just fridge-magnet pacifiers? Quotable axioms to deliver to other people when trouble hits *them*?
Or can I *actually* build resilience according to the pattern of the Bible and truly be able to 'stand strong' in times of difficulty and anguish?

What does *building resilience* actually mean for my day to day life?
For my - sitting in a waiting room waiting for a skin cancer test result - life?

What's the real point of resilience? Is it so that I eventually hit a point in my faith where I have 'made it'? Where I am so strong, so 'Holy' that my entire life is spent walking on clouds and nothing touches my inner peace? Where my decisions are all perfectly in line with God's will and life's troubles simply bounce off my invisible force-field of faith!?

That would be nice, but I don't think so.

*****

Jeremiah, an Old Testament prophet was having a bit of grumble one day, towards God. I love God's reply, which really speaks to the purpose of resilience:

*"If you have raced with men on foot*
*and they have worn you out,*
*how can you compete with horses?*
*If you stumble in safe country,*
*how will you manage in the thickets by the Jordan?"[171]*

Do you hear this?
Can you see the bigger picture of a life of resilience?

God was telling Jeremiah that the point of overcoming the current obstacles in your path, the real point of thriving in times of trouble is so that you are strong enough to face even larger obstacles.
You can handle bigger trouble!
You don't overcome the foot racers in order that you can put your feet up and rest, you beat the foot racers so that you can compete against horses!

Every time you have faced a trial and won; whenever trouble came at you and you stood strong, resilient in the face of difficult odds; each time a challenge threatened to overwhelm you but you put your trust in

164

God and came through it, you were actually preparing yourself for the next thing, training yourself for the *impossible* trial.

Do you get it?

Winning on foot is hard but it's possible. Competing against horses is impossible. If we haven't trained ourselves to trust God, to lean into him and to put our hope in His presence we won't stand a chance.

We need to win on foot first so that we can face the horses with confidence.
I need to have learned that Christ is enough, that His grace is sufficient for me so that the 'horse' of a cancer diagnosis won't overwhelm me

*Consider it a sheer gift, friends, when tests and challenges come at you from all sides. You know that under pressure, your faith-life is forced into the open and shows its true colours. So don't try to get out of anything prematurely. Let it do its work so you become mature and well-developed, not deficient in any way.*[172]

We become mature (and resilient) when we let the troubles of this world do their work.

*****

In the Old Testament book of Samuel, we read about how a boy named David won his early battles, protecting his father's sheep against lions and bears. Now to my mind, beating lions and bears doesn't sound like a simple 'training exercise' but David's future had bigger and more challenging troubles. Had David not learned to trust God in the sheep-field, he wouldn't have stood a hope in the battle-field, against the warrior-giant Goliath.

In the book of Exodus we find Moses, running scared from Egypt and escaping to the wilderness, where he had to become skilled at leading himself, learning patience and trust over the span of forty years before he was ready to lead the nation of Israel out of slavery.

We read in the gospels how Jesus won his own battle against temptation and the devil in the wilderness before he was empowered by the spirit to fulfil his ministry here on earth and bring salvation to a dying world.

We need to face our trials with courage and with a deep trust and conviction that God is with us in the troubles.

I have learned that God will provide the strength I need at the point that I need it to discover a path through the troubles I am facing.

But courage….
Courage is what I need to bring to the party!

Courage is crucial for a thriving life. To be fully devoted followers of Jesus we are going to need courage, the audacity to step out in boldness, to take risks which, from a human standpoint, can seem ridiculous.

Many times throughout the bible we read the commands: 'do not fear', 'don't be afraid', 'be bold', 'have courage',' take heart'. The truth is, fear can be crippling to our soul. It affects our judgement and our choices. It causes us to live smaller lives by avoiding difficult pathways and potential trouble. In this way we can miss opportunities to become mature and resilient.

*****

Before the nation of Israel had kings to lead them, they were led by judges; men and women who were called and appointed to help the nation return from their constant rebellion against God and to provide leadership in battle against hostile invaders.

In one moment during this period, Israel has been occupied by the Midianites. This was a particularly dreadful time for God's chosen people:

*They camped on the land and ruined the crops all the way to Gaza and did not spare a living thing for Israel, neither sheep nor cattle nor donkeys. They came up with their livestock and their tents like swarms of locusts. It was impossible to count them or their camels; they invaded the land to ravage it. Midian so impoverished the Israelites that they cried out to the Lord for help.*[173]

In this time of disaster and great fear we read Gideon's story.

The first picture we have of Gideon is of a young man,

*'threshing wheat in a winepress'.*[174]

These five words tell us everything we need to know about young Gideon's state of mind. To thresh wheat effectively, you need to be in an exposed place where you can toss the wheat into the air with your pitchfork, the wind blows away the lighter chaff and the valuable grain fall to the ground. The winepress was most likely a pit dug into the ground and so was hidden from the Midianites. So, no wind to blow away the chaff. Gideon had essentially sacrificed effectiveness for his own safety and the safety of his crop - which is perfectly reasonable and understandable given the position Israel found themselves in.

However, the next scene that plays out is about to turn Gideon's world on its head.

An angel from God appears to Gideon in this moment and greets him in a rather perplexing manner:

*"The Lord is with you, mighty warrior."*[175] (mighty man of valour, man of fearless courage, mighty hero!)

The question has to be asked, given that Gideon is standing where he is, doing what he is doing: Is the angel being ironic or sarcastic, or is he simply calling out of Gideon something that he doesn't even recognise within himself?

I'm sure that many of us can relate to Gideon's predicament. Our life doesn't feel as effective as we think it could be. We are confident that God has greater things for us, that his plans are bigger for us, and yet we find ourselves in a safe and comfortable place. Desiring God's best, but not sure about stepping out of the safety of the 'winepress'.

Gideon counters by asking a couple of searching questions to the angel (when you've got an angel from God in the room, you might as well make the most of it by verbalising your doubts!). The reply:

*"Go in the strength you have and save Israel out of Midian's hand. Am I not sending you."*[176]

The important word here is not 'strength'.
It's Go.

Go, step out of the winepress, make a move, be bold and courageous. Don't worry about needing more strength, more ability, figuring out the answers. Go with what you've already got. I'm sending you.

Perhaps you think you are not talented enough, not smart enough, not strong enough, you don't have enough time or enough energy, you're too busy or too weak or too flawed. Maybe you are saying, 'I have this burning desire on my mind and a burden in my heart but I don't know how to fulfil it. I can see plenty others who would be better suited to take this on, people who are more qualified than me.'

If that's you, you can take heart that Gideon felt exactly the same:

*"Pardon me, my lord," Gideon replied, "but how can I save Israel? My clan is the weakest in Manasseh, and I am the least in my family."*[177]

I know that you're God and everything but perhaps this time you might have got it wrong. You need to choose a different person. In fact, you need to choose someone from a different family. I think you might even have the wrong church; we couldn't possibly get involved in something so big. Really God, you'd do better finding someone from a different country! We in the U.K. are a little bit timid. The U.S.A! They think much bigger there…perhaps they are more suited to this kind of mission.

How does God respond to Gideon's objections?
'What?! How dare you question my judgement. I'm God! I picked you because you *are* the strongest and the smartest person I could find. You are a natural match for this mission. You have trained all your life for this. You need to trust in your own incredible powers. Now go get 'em!'

No.
He doesn't say that, in case you're wondering

God doesn't enter into a debate or even disagree with anything Gideon says. He doesn't argue with him. He doesn't try and convince Gideon of his merits for the mission. God simply and quietly lays down his trump card:
"I will be with you"[178]

I.

Will.

Be.

With.

You.

Go in the strength you have…I will be with you.

The strength you already have (although it doesn't feel like much) is enough *if* you just have the courage to step out.

Weakness is no barrier, in fact, acknowledging your own weakness is the first step in accomplishing great things. (Remember chapter 3 – I Can't do it?)

This seems to be one of the biggest obstacles to stepping out in courage – the fear that we are not enough, that we're going to fail, that we don't have what it takes to succeed in a particular endeavour.

So, we waste our lives threshing wheat in a winepress, not realising that living your life in a condition devoid of risk is not living at all. We can always find the excuses we need.

\*\*\*\*\*

I mentioned earlier in the book about our firstborn son, whom we called 'Gideon' after this amazing bible character.

A number of years ago, when I had just completed my Performing Arts Degree and my (future) wife and I were paying off our student debt and saving to buy a home and get married, I went to an agency to find temporary work, just until I could find my feet in the heady world of music and the arts. That is how I ended up at The Royal Bank of Scotland in Blackfriars, London. It felt a little bit like selling my soul but on the other hand I needed the money and I *knew* it was only temporary.

Three years later, there I was, still working at the bank, and now I had a wife and a mortgage and all the other assorted bills that come with owning your own home. I knew God had called me to more, specifically in the field of music composition, but I guess the bank became my 'winepress' in which I was 'threshing wheat'.

I remember clearly the day when God spoke to me (not audibly – but through a Sunday message at church) and let me know it was time to hand in my notice at the bank. Unfortunately, God didn't see fit to fill me in with the whole plan. I didn't get a bulleted list of all the action steps I needed to take in order to make this work. Just - 'hand in your notice.'

Which I did.
The very next day. After a difficult chat with my wife (who was, as ever, gracious and faith-filled!)

Six weeks to find a new job. My search began in earnest. I researched through journals and the Yellow Pages (remember those), through Job ads and various contacts. (Remember, these were the 'dark ages' before Google was even a twinkle in its founders' eyes.) I printed off more than a hundred letters and application forms for jobs in the music industry. I had them all neatly stacked, stamped and addressed in hand-written envelopes.

That's when God spoke to me again (not audibly – but through the bible), specifically through this story of Gideon. I'm sure you all know how it works out. Gideon raises an army of thirty-two thousand men. All armed and ready to do battle with the evil Midianites. God tells Gideon that he has too many men because if they win, they will get the credit and not God. Over the course of a couple of tests, God whittles Gideon's army down to a meagre three hundred men and announces:

*"With the three hundred men...I will save you and give the Midianites into your hands."*[179]

In this critical moment that Gideon is at his weakest, and his army is, let's face it, nominal, God is ready for business.

So, there was I, ready for action with my army of applications and envelopes and, after reading this account of Gideon, that small voice in my spirit asks me, 'If you send all these applications, who will get the credit when you get a new job?'

Ouch!
Really God?
What do you want me to do?
I'm obviously not just going to throw them all in the bin.
Am I?

So, after another 'chat' with my ever patient and faith-filled wife, I threw them in the bin.
Obviously.

And I waited.
And waited some more.

Two weeks, three weeks, four weeks, five weeks go by and nothing.
And I am waiting.
And praying quite hard.

Two days before my six-week notice period has expired, my wife is on a train and strikes up a conversation with a vague acquaintance, who explains that he is looking for someone to help him run his music and instrument distribution company.

Fortunately, she knew just the person...

*****

Imagine for a moment the courage and faith it took for Gideon to go into battle against the Midianites (who were numbered like swarms of locusts), having had his army decimated from thirty-two thousand to three hundred. All because God didn't want Israel to say 'My own strength saved me'.

And imagine also for a moment, Gideon and his army, at the end of the battle, exhausted and exhilarated at having defeated the Midianite multitude against all odds. Knowing in a much deeper sense that God was with them and he wouldn't ever let them down.

My own 'Gideon' episode was a defining moment in my life (hence the name of our firstborn).
It grew my faith and courage.
It taught me obedience.
It felt like an impossible win at the time but of course I now realise that this was simply racing on foot and the races against horses were to come.
I also realised that this is 'bread and butter' to the God I worship and serve.
There are no impossible races for Him.

(Just in case you are interested, two days after my wife's 'chance' meeting on a train, I found myself on a plane to Frankfurt, attending one of the world's largest music shows. For the next twelve years, I worked as a full-time musician/composer and God provided everything my family needed.)

Following God's plan will hardly ever be easy, but we can trust that our omnipresent, omniscient and omnipotent God will continue to equip us, guide us and strengthen us in whatever battles and circumstances we have the courage to find ourselves.

*****

Which brings me back to my own cancer diagnosis.

Today is Monday.
On Wednesday I'm being admitted into hospital for surgery.

The battles I have already faced and overcome have brought me to this moment.

I have peace.

I have faith in a sovereign, awesome and caring God.

I guess this is the whole point of resilience.
To be able to face the next challenge with hope and faith.
Whatever the outcome.

[1] John 16:33(b) NIV

[2] John 16:33 (b) The Amplified Bible

[3] John 16:33 NIV

[4] 1 Cor 15:9-10

[5] Ps. 73:26

[6] Eph 2:3-4

[7] Romans 6:14

[8] John 16:33 NIV

[9] Fred Rogers, The World According to Mister Rogers: Important Things to Remember

[10] Cambridge Dictionary. Cambridge University Press. 2020

[11] Matthew 5 to 7

[12] Matthew 7:24a Peterson, Eugene H. *The Message.* Colorado Springs, CO: NavPress, 2002. Print.

[13] Matthew 7:24b – 25 Peterson, Eugene H. *The Message.* Colorado Springs, CO: NavPress, 2002. Print.

[14] John 16:33a

[15] Matthew 7:26-27 Peterson, Eugene H. *The Message.* Colorado Springs, CO: NavPress, 2002. Print.

[16] *The Collected Letters of C. S. Lewis, Volume II: Family Letters 1905-1931.* Copyright © 2004 by C. S. Lewis Pte. Ltd.

[17] John 10:10b

[18] Job 17:9 (NLT)

[19] Composed by Bill Conti

[20] Genesis 50:19-20 NIV

[21] Genesis 41:16 NIV

[22] James 4:6b NIV

[23] Hebrews 4:16 NIV

[24] Hebrews 13:6 NIV

[25] 1 Peter 5:6 NIV

[26] Romans 8:28, 31b, 35, 37 NIV

[27] Genesis 48:20b NIV

[28] John 16:33 (emphasis mine)

[29] Hebrews 13:6

[30] Joshua 1:9

[31] Ephesians 6:11

[32] Haggai 2:5

[33] Matthew 21:21

[34] Hebrews 11:1

[35] John Guare. Landscape of the body.

[36] Proverbs 11:7 NIV

[37] Matthew 10:30 NIV

[38] Psalm 23:1,4a

[39] Psalm 23:5

[40] Matthew 8:6

[41] Matthew 8:7 NIV

[42] Matthew 8:8a NIV

[43] Matthew 8:8b NIV

[44] Matthew 8:9a

[45] Matthew 8:10 NIV

[46] Hebrews 6:13-18 The Message

[47] Hebrews 6:19 NIV

[48] Jeremiah 6:14 The Message

[49] Psalm 39:2-3 The Message

[50] Ephesians 4:31-32

[51] Matthew 18:21 NIV

[52] Matthew 18:22

[53] Galatians 1:10

[54] 1 Corinthians 15:9

[55] Ephesians 3:8

[56] 1 Timothy 1:15

[57] Matthew 18:32-35

[58] Romans 12:19

[59] Bruce Almighty (2003)

[60] Romans 12:20

[61] Jeremiah 31:34

[62] Psalm 61:1-3

[63] Isaiah 61:1-3

[64] John 16:33a

[65] John 16:33b

[66] Hebrews 13:15

[67] John 14:6

[68] Psalm 57:9

[69] Acts 16:16-18

[70] Acts 16:22-24

[71] Acts 16:25

[72] Psalm 54 NIV

[73] Exodus 15:20-21

[74] Artist: Tim McGraw. Writer: Sean McConnell. Copyright Warner Chappell Music Inc.

[75] 2 Chronicles 20:15b,17a

[76] 2 Chronicles 20:18-19

[77] 2 Chronicles 20:21-22

[78] Daniel 3:16-18

[79] Raise a Hallelujah. Jonathon David Helser and Melissa Helser

[80] Psalm 34:1-3

[81] Matthew chapters 5-7

[82] Matthew 5:3-12

[83] Deuteronomy 28:1-14

[84] Deuteronomy 28:15-68

[85] Deuteronomy 29:1a

[86] Genesis 17:7

[87] Luke 22:20b

[88] Romans 4:7-8

[89] 2 Corinthians 5:21

[90] Romans 10:9

[91] Romans 12:3

[92] Matthew 7:4 NIV

[93] I Can See Clearly Now. Johnny Nash. 1972

[94] Michael Jackson. Man in the Mirror.

[95] 1 Tim 6:10

[96] Romans 12:2

[97] 1 Peter 5:8-9

[98] Luke 12:15 ESV

[99] Philippians 4:12-13

[100] Matthew 25:23

[101] Luke 21:3

[102] Luke 19:8-9

[103] Acts 4:32

[104] Genesis 12:1-3

[105] 2 Corinthians 9:8

[106] 2 Corinthians 9:11

[107] Luke 6:38

[108] Proverbs 11:24 The Message

[109] Proverbs 3:9-10

[110] 1 Corinthians 16:1-3

[111] Malachi 3:8-12

[112] John 17:20-23

[113] John 10:10

[114] James 4:6

[115] Matthew 12:25

[116] Acts 2:2-4

[117] Acts 2:9-11

[118] Galatians 3:26-28

[119] Acts 2:42-47

[120] Acts 1:8b

[121] Ephesians 2:21

[122] Psalm 133

[123] Matthew 18:19-20

[124] 1 Thessalonians 5:11

[125] 1 Thessalonians 5:16-18

[126] 1 Corinthains 12:12-14

[127] Mark 3:25

[128] 1 Corinthians 12:26

[129] John 17:23b

[130] Galatians 5:13b

[131] John 13:1

[132] John 13:3-17

[133] Matthew 20:26

[134] Philippians 2:3-4

[135] Philippians 2:6-8

[136] Philippians 2:5

[137] John 14:12

[138] John 1:26-27

[139] John 13:6-8

[140] John 13:8b-9

[141] John 13:10

[142] John 13:17

[143] San Andreas. (2015)

[144] The Best Exotic Marigold Hotel. (2011)

[145] Matthew 14:21

[146] Matthew 14:25-33

[147] Mark 6:47-48a (emphasis mine)

[148] Mark 6:48b (emphasis mine)

[149] 2002 Reuben Morgan/Hillsong Publishing

[150] Eric Oskar Liljero / Jonas Carl Gustaf Myrin / Reuben Timothy Morgan

[151] James 1:2-4

[152] Deuteronomy 31:6, Joshua 1:9, 1 Chronicles 28:20, John 14:27, 1 Corinthians 16:13

[153] Matthew 14:28

[154] John Ortberg. If You Want to Walk on Water, You've Got to Get Out of the Boat. 2001.

[155] Mark 10:21b

[156] Matthew 14:30

[157] Matthew 14:31

[158] Matthew 14:32a

[159] The Next Right Thing lyrics © Universal Music Publishing Group

[160] Psalm 71:14

[161] Psalm 71:15-21

[162] Joshua 24:15

[163] Genesis 24:12

[164] Genesis 24:26-27

[165] Psalm 119:105

[166] 1 Samuel 12:1-2

[167] 1 Samuel 12:23

[168] Psalm 73

[169] Psalm 73:23-28

[170] Winston S. Churchill

[171] Jeremiah 12:5

[172] James 1:2-4

[173] Judges 6:4-6

[174] Judges 6:11

[175] Judges 6:12

[176] Judges 6:14

[177] Judges 6:15

[178] Judges 6:16

[179] Judges 7:7

Printed in Great Britain
by Amazon

49918894R00108